Five-Minute Activities for Young Learners

Cambridge Handbooks for Language Teachers

This is a series of practical guides for teachers of English and other languages. Illustrative examples are usually drawn from the field of English as a foreign or second language, but the ideas and techniques described can equally well be used in the teaching of any language.

Recent titles in this series:

Five-Minute Activities for Young Learners

Penny McKay and Jenni Guse

CAMBRIDGE
UNIVERSITY PRESS

CAMBRIDGE UNIVERSITY PRESS
Cambridge, New York, Melbourne, Madrid, Cape Town, Singapore, São Paulo, Delhi

Cambridge University Press
The Edinburgh Building, Cambridge CB2 8RU, UK

www.cambridge.org
Information on this title: www.cambridge.org/9780521691345

© Cambridge University Press 2007

It is normally necessary for written permission for copying to be
obtained *in advance* from a publisher. Certain parts of this book are
designed to be copied and distributed in class. The normal requirements
are waived here and it is not necessary to write to Cambridge University
Press for permission for an individual teacher to make copies for use within
his or her own classroom. Only those pages which carry the wording
'© Cambridge University Press 2007' may be copied.

First published 2007
Reprinted 2008

Printed in the United Kingdom at the University Press, Cambridge

A catalogue record for this publication is available from the British Library

Library of Congress Cataloging-in-Publication Data
McKay, Penny
   Five-minute activities for young learners / Penny McKay and Jenni Guse.
      p. cm. — (Cambridge handbooks for language teachers)
   Includes bibliographical references and index.
   ISBN 978-0-521-69134-5 (pbk.)
   1. English language—Study and teaching (Elementary)—Foreign
speakers—Activity programs.   I. Guse, Jenni.   II. Title.
   PE1128.A2M388   2007
   372.6´044—dc22

                                                            2006100690

ISBN 978-0-521-69134-5 paperback

Cambridge University Press has no responsibility for the persistence or
accuracy of URLs for external or third-party internet websites referred to in
this publication, and does not guarantee that any content on such websites is,
or will remain, accurate or appropriate.

Contents

Contents

Contents

Thanks and Acknowledgements

The authors would like to thank their partners, Andy and Allan, for their support during their teaching and more recently their writing. They would like to give special thanks to Scott Thornbury for his expert guidance in the shaping of the material in this book.

They would also like to thank Frances Amrani, Roslyn Henderson and Hilary Ratcliff for their very expert and supportive editorial work.

Introduction

Purpose, scope and use of this book

This book is designed to provide short, topical and achievable teaching ideas for teachers of English to young learners, whether they are following a required syllabus or textbook, or preparing a curriculum that is targeted at their own group of learners. The particular value of the book is that it provides teachers with a store of activities that they can use, at long or short notice, to meet a specific learning objective, or to fill a gap (or reinforce a learning point) that becomes apparent as children study the scheduled curriculum or textbook. When chosen carefully by the teacher to suit the current theme and to meet the planned objectives, the activities in this book can be used in several ways. They can act as supplementary mainstay activities in the planned curriculum to support the progress of learning already underway. They can also act as reinforcement activities if children need to focus a little more on a particular aspect of learning. And (so long as their use is consistent with the overall teaching goals) they can be used simply to liven up the class, to inject interest or adrenalin, and to give the children five minutes of fun. We recommend that you keep this book at your side when you do your planning, and handy when teaching, ready for those moments when children need reinforcement, or have shown that they can take on another quick challenge.

The audience for this book

The audience for this book is teachers of English to children aged from six to twelve years of age. They may be teachers of EFL (English as a Foreign Language) or ESL/EAL (English as a Second Language / English as an Additional Language). EFL teachers are teaching English in a situation where English is seldom heard outside the classroom. ESL teachers are teaching English to children who are learning English as the main language of communication and learning in their classrooms, school and community. For both EFL and ESL teachers, the activities in this book can be used as mainstay or supplementary reinforcement activities.

In a mainstream ESL context, we are assuming that, as much as possible, the ESL teacher will try to relate the activities to the content of mainstream classes. For example, you may choose a five-minute activity to correspond with a science topic from a mainstream class. This activity will not only meet specific language objectives, but may also provide a link between the language classroom and the mainstream class. Similarly, if the children are learning about narratives in their mainstream classes, you, the language teacher, could choose a number of five-minute activities which focus on the language features of narratives. In this way, language teachers can help to build an integrated curriculum, while at the same time catering for different levels of ability, skills and content knowledge.

The structure of this book

We have organised the book into six themes, and each theme contains activities which have been divided into three levels of difficulty: one star (*) represents the lowest level of difficulty, while three stars (***) represent the most challenging activities. The box at the top of each activity also contains the Language focus and Skills focus for each activity, along with a Thinking focus and suggestions for the teacher about accepting or correcting errors. The nature of the interaction, i.e. group work, pairwork, etc. is noted at the top of each activity, and the teacher's preparation for each activity is also clearly stated.

The six themes in this book have been chosen to appeal to both boys and girls from a wide age range. The topics, which relate to common learning topics in EFL and ESL classrooms, are usually covered in young learner EFL tests (for example, the Cambridge Young Learners English Test) and in many course books. The topics also underpin learning in the curriculum in most primary mainstream classrooms. They are as follows:

Animals
Journeys
Fantasy and adventure
The world around us
Healthy bodies
About me

The design of the activities allows teachers to adapt and apply the ideas to other themes. Teachers may decide to use the activities for five to ten minutes, or it is possible for experienced teachers to extend a number of activities and adapt these for more able students.

The philosophy underpinning the activities

We have structured the book so that it encourages meaningful language use and real communication appropriate to primary age learners and their learning contexts. Even when children are practising vocabulary, pronunciation or language structures, they do so in a meaningful way, in an activity where their own meanings are created, supported and exchanged with others. The arrangement in themes is important because it enables children to build up a store of topic-related language items that they can recycle as they move on to more advanced activities on the same topic. We have used a range of genres, such as recount, information report, procedure, narrative, explanation and argument, to provide a range of contexts and purposes for language use.

From our knowledge of child development (including an appreciation of multiple intelligences) and from a desire to focus on individual learners, we have created activities that are hands-on and appeal to a child's sense of fun. Such activities are enjoyable and achievable and motivate learners because they enable them to be successful according to their individual abilities. We have involved movement, active participation and games. A spiral model which recycles language, together with an awareness of higher-order thinking skills, has enabled us to cater for children's cognitive development. (The spiralling of learning depends, of course, to a large extent, on the order in which teachers choose activities.)

Through the activities, we aim to enable children to think and to communicate in English, so that as they acquire new language, they develop strategies to communicate, and are then able to apply this new knowledge to new situations. Through this process, then, children are able to learn how language is organised, used and learned. We have also aimed to give children an opportunity to reflect on and learn new things as they participate in the activities.

The content of the activities

The activities focus on the four macro skills, listening, speaking, reading and writing, and the 'building blocks' of language, vocabulary, pronunciation and grammar. They also focus on developing learning strategies, for example, certain decoding strategies to enhance reading skills, pronunciation strategies to aid clear oral language, and higher-order thinking skills (such as categorising, classifying, defining, explaining, drawing conclusions, hypothesising, making connections between ideas, and considering multiple viewpoints or conflicting views) to improve children's thinking abilities.

Materials needed

We assume that teachers have a blackboard and chalk, or whiteboard and marker, for every activity. Other materials that teachers need are listed.

We encourage teachers to display children's work around the classroom. Lists of words, and pictures, and other material that is used in the activities can also be used for display. Displays give children a chance to revisit what they have learned, and when they look around the classroom they can feel good about what they have done. Teachers can also organise children to keep their 'activity work' in a book or portfolio in which they stick or keep their work, and to which they return from time to time.

Class sizes

In designing the activities, we have been mindful that children learn English in many different settings, ranging from small groups to large classes. The activities are flexible enough to cater for English teaching and learning in a variety of contexts.

How to choose activities

You are free to use any activity and in any order, but, according to good teaching practice, you should always consider whether children are ready for this activity or whether it would be better to do a less advanced activity, or to do an earlier activity in the sequence of activities. If you choose a number of activities in one level in one theme, then there is more opportunity for recycling and consolidation of learning.

There are many ways to fit these five-minute activities into schemes of work; ideas will easily arise as teachers read the many activities, and keep in mind their objectives and their children's needs. The five-minute activities can act as a planned activity for one of the teaching phases, they can be slotted in as the teacher realises the need for more focus or reinforcement during the scheme of work, or they can be picked up and used because the children enjoyed them and they help them to review past learning once the scheme of work is finished.

How to fit a five-minute activity into an overall scheme of work

Scheme of work in an EFL context: writing to a friend in another classroom about the things in their classroom

In this example, this five-minute activity is a mainstay activity embedded in a scheme of work in which EFL children are writing a letter to a friend describing their classroom. Remember that there is not always a clear distinction between EFL and ESL activities; these types of activities might also be used in intensive ESL contexts where the ESL teacher is planning and teaching the activities directly, focussing more on language and preparing children for mainstream learning.

1 Preparation phase of scheme of work: activating lexis about things in the classroom (see box below).
2 Core phase of scheme of work: producing sentences – orally and then in writing – about things around them.
3 Follow-up phase: writing a letter to a friend describing their classroom.

The five-minute activity can also be used later during the scheme of work as a reinforcement activity, say at the beginning of a new lesson during the scheme of work, or during a spare five minutes in classroom activities.

6.2 My classroom (five-minute activity used as a Preparation phase)

Level	*
Language focus	Vocabulary: classroom objects
Skills focus	Listening for details
Thinking focus	Following directions
Teaching approach	Promote accuracy – correct errors
Interaction	Whole class work, suitable for large classes
Preparation	On small slips of paper, write the names of a number of familiar classroom items. Choose objects from the basic game. See Box 112. Jumble these and put them into a container.

Procedure

1 Ask each child to choose one object from the classroom and place it on his/her desk.
2 Then ask the children to stand and listen to the names of the objects as you draw them out of the container.
3 As you select a slip of paper, read out the name of the object. Anyone with this object has to sit down.
4 Continue to draw out all the slips of paper one by one, and read out the name of the object. The last children left standing are the winners.
5 It is possible that some children have chosen objects which you did not include in your list. If they know the English word for these items, then they win bonus points.

Box 112   Classroom objects

Classroom objects: basic game	Classroom objects: advanced game
Book	*Add one adjective:*
Pen	Red pencil
Picture	Old toy
Eraser	Tennis ball
Pencil	
Ruler	*Add two adjectives:*
Ball	New English book
Game	Big picture book
Toy	Old test book
Bag	
Box	

Scheme of work in an ESL mainstream context: beginning a scheme of work on space travel

In this example, in an ESL mainstream context, the teacher is using this five-minute activity to give her/his advanced ESL learners an opportunity to become familiar with the language of space travel, the new theme being studied by the mainstream class. The ESL learners need to know more than vocabulary – they need to know how to discern and express strengths and weaknesses in an argument, which in turn involves the language of creative thinking (analysing, contrasting, evaluating). A well-prepared teacher will also be aware that these ESL learners need support to establish their understanding about space travel. So the five-minute activity can help the children to prepare their thoughts for the scheme of work, while at the same time helping them check their ideas through oral language (as in this activity) with their teacher and their classmates. Through this kind of activity, the ESL learners are therefore being given a chance to learn and apply some of the English vocabulary they need to talk about travel in space. They are also learning ways to talk about strengths and weaknesses. They are doing this in a sharing and fun classroom situation with their mainstream classmates, or at least with their more advanced ESL classmates before they join the main class. This will help them to join in with other whole class activities as the mainstream scheme of work on space travel progresses.

2.17 Holidays in space

Level	***
Language focus	Debate, modal expressions
Skills focus	Speaking
Thinking focus	Analysing, contrasting and evaluating
Teaching approach	Promote creativity – accept errors
Interaction	Whole class, suitable for large classes
	Group discussion
Preparation	Draw a large grid on the board. See Box 42.

Procedure

1 Write the topic on the board: *Holidays in space*.
2 Refer to the large grid on the board.
3 Tell the children that you want them to think of the advantages and disadvantages of having a holiday in space. Give them an example of the sort of ideas that can appear in each section of the grid. See Box 43 for suggestions.
4 Divide the class into teams, and each team has a turn to add one idea to the strengths and weaknesses grid. Team members discuss their answers first and then choose one idea to add to the grid. Encourage the children to use the modal expressions *could/couldn't*, *might*, *would* and *may*. They continue until they run out of ideas.
5 The team to contribute the last idea is the winner.

Box 42   Space travel: strengths and weaknesses grid

Topic: Holidays in space	
Strengths	**Weaknesses**

Box 43   Questions about space travel

Strengths

Teacher: What are the good things about going on a holiday into space? What would we enjoy? How would we benefit?

Children: It's a new experience. We could see things we've never seen before, e.g. Saturn's rings, Mars' volcano. We could see the Earth from space. We might meet other friendly life forms. We might learn about how the solar system was formed.

Weaknesses

Teacher: What are some of the problems we could face? What would stop us from going on a holiday in space?

Children: It's too expensive. We would be away for a long time. We couldn't eat our normal food. It's too hot / too cold. There could be angry aliens in space. The space ship may break down.

The scheme of work will continue with a range of other science and creative writing and group work activities around the space travel theme, and will continue to draw on children to express their oral and written ideas about strengths and weaknesses (analysing, contrasting, evaluating) in the space travel theme.

1 Animals

1.1 What animals do you know?

Level	*
Language focus	Vocabulary: animal names
Skills focus	Writing
Thinking focus	Classifying
Teaching approach	Promote creativity – accept errors
Interaction	Group work or pairs, suitable for large classes

Procedure

1 Form the class into groups. Each group has a large sheet of paper. In large classes, students could work in pairs, each with a sheet of paper.
2 Children write as many animals as they can think of in one minute.
3 They then pass the large sheet of paper to the group on their right or to the pair on their right.
4 The children read their peers' suggestions and add more animals to the list.
5 Continue rotating the sheet of paper until it returns to the original group. In large classes, pass the paper round five pairs.
6 Create a summary grid on the board, using the headings from Box 1.
7 Ask the students to call out the name of an animal that falls into the following categories: Farm animals, Pets, and Wild animals, and record these into the grid.

Box 1 Animal names

Farm animals	Pets	Wild animals
chicken, cow, duck, goat, horse, sheep	bird, cat, dog, fish, horse, mouse	bird, crocodile, duck, elephant, fish, frog, giraffe, hippo, lizard, monkey, mouse, snake, spider, tiger

Follow-up

The children copy the name of each animal onto a playing card. They can then play card games such as Snap and Concentration. See Box 2 for instructions on how to play these card games.

Box 2   Card games

These games are best played in groups of two to four players.

Snap

- Divide the cards between the players.
- Each player takes a turn to place a card on the table, thus revealing the content of the card.
- When two cards match, e.g. if there are two pets (e.g. a cat and a dog) or two farm animals (e.g. a cow and a horse), the first person to place a hand over the pack and say *Snap* wins all these cards.
- The game continues until one player has won all the cards.

Concentration

- All the cards are placed face down spread out on the table.
- Each player takes a turn to choose two cards.
- If the cards make a pair, e.g. if there are two farm animals, the player keeps the cards and has another turn.
- If there is no pair, the cards are replaced, face down, in the same position.
- The game continues until all pairs have been claimed.

1.2   Describing well-known animals

Level	*
Language focus	Vocabulary: adjectives
Skills focus	Listening and writing
Thinking focus	Selecting and defining
Teaching approach	Promote accuracy – correct errors
Interaction	Pairwork, suitable for large classes
Preparation	Draw a grid on the board. Write the headings, but no details. See Box 3.

Procedure

1 Read out the name of one animal from Box 3 that the children will recognise, e.g. *Frog*.
2 The children write down the name of the animal, paying attention to correct spelling.
3 Ask the children, in pairs, to think of physical characteristics of this animal, e.g. *Small, soft, wet, green*. Encourage the children to use classroom wallcharts, dictionaries or classroom books to find suitable describing words. Suggested vocabulary is in Box 3. Call on the children to share their answers with the class.
4 Complete the grid on the board.

Box 3   Describing animals

Animal	Size	Colour	Touch
frog	small	green	cool, wet
snake	long	black, brown, green	smooth, cool
elephant	big	grey	hard
fish	small/big	silver, grey, red, blue, gold, orange	wet, cool

---

1.3 Animals moving about

Level	*
Language focus	Action verbs, *can*
Skills focus	Speaking
Thinking focus	Memorising
Teaching approach	Promote creativity – accept errors
Interaction	Whole class work, suitable for large classes

Procedure

1 Choose one child to select a favourite animal, e.g. *A fish*.
2 Ask him/her *What can your animal do?*, e.g. *Swim*.
3 Write on the board *I am a fish and I can swim*.

4 Ask the child to read this sentence aloud. This child then selects someone else to choose a favourite animal.

5 The next child chooses an animal and says e.g. *He is a fish and he can swim. I am a monkey and I can climb.* This child selects someone else to choose a favourite animal.

6 The third child chooses an animal and says e.g. *He is a fish and he can swim. She is a monkey and she can climb. I am a bird and I can fly.*

7 The game continues for as long as the children can think of animals and remember the previous contributions.

1.4 Animal rhythms

Level	*
Language focus	Vocabulary: animal names
Skills focus	Speaking, pronunciation: rhythm and stress
Thinking focus	Recognising
Teaching approach	Promote accuracy – correct errors
Interaction	Whole class work, suitable for large classes
Preparation	Choose one animal from each of the columns and write their names on the board. See Box 4.

Procedure

1 Clap out the rhythm of the name of one animal from the board, e.g. Three claps could be *e–le–phant*.

2 The children try to identify the animal from the list of names on the board.

3 The children then read and clap the rhythm of this animal.

4 Ask them if they know of any other animals that have a similar stress pattern. Practise saying and clapping the names and rhythms.

5 Choose a child to clap out another rhythm and ask the class to guess the animal. To extend this activity, you may want to focus on the stress patterns for each animal, as well as the rhythm. A list of animals and stress patterns are in Box 4.

Box 4   Names of animals

One syllable	Two syllables: stress on the first syllable	Two syllables: stress on the second syllable	Three syllables: stress on the first syllable	Three syllables: stress on the middle syllable	Three syllables: stress on the first and last syllable
cow	chicken	giraffe	elephant	mosquito	kangaroo
bird	lizard	gazelle	crocodile	koala	polar bear
cat	tiger	baboon			
duck	hippo				
dog	monkey				
frog	spider				
goat					
horse					
mouse					
sheep					
snake					

Follow-up

Make a chart of animal names and stress patterns. Each time the children come across another animal name, e.g. in a book they are currently reading, ask them to add it to the chart.

1.5 Singing about animals

Level	*
Language focus	Song, vocabulary: animal names
Skills focus	Speaking: pronunciation
Thinking focus	Ranking
Teaching approach	Promote accuracy – correct errors
Interaction	Whole class work, suitable for large classes

Procedure

1 Introduce the song *Old Macdonald had a farm*.
2 Ask the children to suggest which animals to sing about, but they must be ranked in order of size, starting with the smallest animal.

3 Write the children's suggestions on the board in a grid. See Box 5.
4 Then ask the children to identify the sound that these animals make. Add these to the grid.
5 Finally, ask the class to sing their new version of *Old Macdonald had a farm.*

Box 5 Animal sizes and sounds

Animals ranked according to size	Sound that the animal makes
1 Bee	Buzz, buzz / Hum, hum
2 Mouse	Squeak, squeak
3 Hen	Cluck, cluck
4 Dog	Woof, woof
5 Pig	Grunt, grunt / Oink, oink
6 Cow	Moo, moo

Follow-up
For other songs, see Activities 2.14, 5.4, 6.7.

1.6 Writing an animal Haiku

Level	*
Language focus	Poem, simple sentences, question forms, present tense, adjectives
Skills focus	Writing: joint construction
Thinking focus	Creating
Teaching approach	Promote creativity – accept errors
Interaction	Whole class, suitable for large classes
Preparation	Select suitable Haiku poems from the website on page 148.

Procedure

1 Choose an animal to be the subject of the class poem, e.g. *A frog.*
2 Ask the class questions about the animal. See Box 6.
3 To construct a Haiku together, the children answer the questions.
4 Write the class Haiku on the board, using the children's answers. See Box 6 for a sample Haiku.
5 Ask the children to recite their class poem together.

Box 6   Creating a Haiku

How to create a Haiku	Example of a Haiku	Information about Haiku
What does the frog feel like to touch? Wet, cold. **What colour is it?** Green. **What does the frog do?** It jumps and opens its mouth. **What does the frog say?** Croak! **What does the frog eat?** Flies for dinner!	**The class Haiku looks like this:** *The wet, cold, green frog. It jumps and opens its mouth. Croak! Flies for dinner!*	Traditionally, Haiku poetry is based on three lines, with the first and last consisting of five syllables, and the middle line consisting of seven syllables. This is not always possible in English, but provides a useful guide to writing Haiku.

Follow-up
- Encourage the children to write their own Haiku by choosing another animal. They could illustrate it and display it in the classroom.
- For other poems and tongue twisters, see Activities 4.5, 6.17.

1.7 Wild animals

Level	**
Language focus	Information report, definitions, simple present tense
Skills focus	Speaking
Thinking focus	Classifying
Teaching approach	Promote accuracy – correct errors
Interaction	Whole class work, suitable for large classes
Preparation	On the board, write the sentence stems from Box 7.

Procedure
1 Ask around the class for examples of animals in the wild. These can range from insects to mammals, from fish to birds, from reptiles to amphibians.
2 Each child in the class contributes an animal until they cannot think of any others. Write all the suggestions randomly on the board.

3 Taking a coloured pen or piece of chalk, circle two animals which belong in the same category, e.g. a pig and a cat are mammals. Then ask the children to suggest another animal that should be circled in this colour, e.g. a mouse. If they cannot think of any, then keep circling mammals until the children understand the reason for your choice.

4 Ask the children to use the sentence stems on the board to tell you why all these animals belong together. See Box 7.

5 Then choose a different colour and circle an animal in a different category, e.g. an insect.

6 Ask the children to choose other animals which fall into this category. When they give their answer, ask them to tell you why they have chosen this animal. (See Note.) The activity continues until all the children's suggestions have been categorised with different coloured circles.

Box 7   Animal classification

Insect	Mammal	Fish	Bird	Reptile	Amphibian	Sentence stems
Small animal Six legs	Gives birth Gives milk to its babies Warm-blooded	Cold-blooded Vertebrate, i.e. has a skeleton or a back bone Lays eggs Lives in water Scales Tail	Has feathers and wings Most birds can fly	Cold-blooded Lays eggs Vertebrate, i.e. has a skeleton or a back bone Scales	Lives in water and on land (Only use the classification *amphibian* if *frog* is one of the suggestions.)	It has . . . It is . . . It lays . . . It can . . . It lives . . . It gives . . .

Note: If students use their first language to describe a skeleton, this gives you the opportunity to introduce new vocabulary such as *vertebrate*, *skeleton* or *back bone*. Children at this level may have been exposed to these concepts in their mainstream classes, but do not have the English language to express their ideas. This is an ideal time to include vocabulary that the children really want to use.

Follow-up
- You could record this classification of animals on a wallchart.
- Children could try to come up with a definition for each category of animal, based on their knowledge of the animals in that category. Their definitions could be added to the wallchart of classified animals. Suggestions are in Box 7.
- For other information reports, see Activities 1.8, 1.13, 2.8, 2.18, 4.14.

1.8 What animal am I?

Level	* *
Language focus	Information report: simple present tense, adjectives
Skills focus	Writing
Thinking focus	Classifying
Teaching approach	Promote creativity – accept errors
Interaction	Whole class, suitable for large classes
Preparation	On the board, draw the grid with headings, questions, and sentence stems. See Box 8.

Procedure
1 Ask the children to write the name of a favourite animal.
2 The children use the headings, questions and sentence stems on the board to write clues about their chosen animal. Examples of clues are in Box 9.
3 Select one child to read out his/her clues.
4 The first person to guess the animal has a turn to read out his/her clues.

Box 8   Animal features

Description	Habitat	Food	Habits	Sentence stems
What do you look like?	Where do you live?	What do you eat?	What can you do?	I am . . . I eat . . . I can . . . I give . . . I live . . .

Box 9   Animal clues

I am brown.
I eat fruit.
I can fly.
I give milk to my babies.
I live in trees.
Who am I? (A fruit bat)

I am yellow and hairy.
I live in grasslands.
I eat other animals.
Who am I? (A lion)

Follow-up
- When children have finished the guessing game, they could classify all their animals, using the categories in Box 7.
- For other information reports, see Activities 1.7, 1.13, 2.8, 2.18, 4.14.

1.9 Guess the animal in 20 questions

Level	* *
Language focus	*Yes/No* questions, simple present tense
Skills focus	Speaking: pronunciation
Thinking focus	Differentiating
Teaching approach	Promote accuracy – correct pronunciation errors
Interaction	Whole class, suitable for large classes
Preparation	On the board, draw the grid with headings and questions. See Box 8. Write the sentence stems from Box 10.

Procedure
1 Choose a child to come to the front of the class.
2 This child decides on an animal. Check that it is a suitable choice for the game.
3 Children in the class create *Yes/No* questions, using the categories from Box 8 and the sentence stems from Box 10. Make sure that the questions can only be answered with *Yes* or *No*. Demonstrate the upward inflection at the end of the question that signals a *Yes/No* question.
4 Whoever guesses the animal has the next turn. If nobody can guess in 20 questions, then the child at the front of the class wins a point.

Box 10   Questions about animals

Sample questions	Sentence stems
1 Do you live near water?	Do you live . . .
2 Do you eat grass?	Do you eat . . .
3 Do you give milk to your babies?	Do you give . . .
4 Can you fly?	Do you have . . .
5 Can you swim?	Can you . . .
	Are you . . .

Follow-up

Encourage the children to include classification terms in their questions, e.g.
Are you a mammal? See Box 7 for animal classification terms.

1.10 Personal animal recount

Level	* *
Language focus	Personal recount, simple past tense
Skills focus	Writing
Thinking focus	Sequencing
Teaching approach	Promote creativity – accept errors
Interaction	Individual work, suitable for large classes

Procedure

1   Ask the children to choose an animal and think about the things that this
animal does during the day.
2   Draw a timeline on the board and write some time markers on the
timeline, e.g. *8 am, 10 am, 12 noon*. See Box 11.
3   Ask the children to copy the timeline.
4   Then ask the children to write in the things that their animal might do
during the day, taking care to write the verb in the past tense. The
completed timelines are then displayed in the classroom.

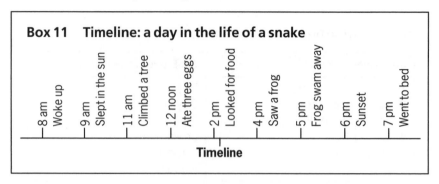

Box 11   Timeline: a day in the life of a snake

Follow-up
- Students could transfer this information into a written or an oral personal recount. A sample of a personal recount is in Box 12.
- For other personal recounts, see Activities 2.13, 2.15, 4.17.

Box 12   Example of a personal recount

Personal recount
A day in the life of a carpet snake
Yesterday I woke up at about 8 am. At 9 o'clock I found a sunny spot, so I took a morning nap. I slept for two hours. After I woke up, I looked for something to eat. I saw a bird's nest in a tree and I climbed up to the nest. I ate three eggs. From 2 pm to 4 pm I looked for food. Next I found a small frog. When the frog saw me it jumped into the pond and swam away. Then the sun set, so I went back to my hole in the rock for the night. I felt hungry and tired.

1.11 Animal raps

Level	**
Language focus	Rap, simple present tense
Skills focus	Speaking: pronunciation – final sounds, rhythm
Thinking focus	Creating
Teaching approach	Promote accuracy – correct pronunciation errors
Interaction	Whole class and group work, suitable for large classes
Preparation	Write the sample rap from Box 13 on the board.

Procedure

1 Introduce the sample rap from Box 13.
2 Ask the children to chant the rap in rhythm, paying attention to the final *s* sound. The stressed syllables are in bold.
3 Write some other possibilities for raps on the board. Suggestions are in Box 13. Groups of children try to write their own rap.
4 The children perform their completed raps to the class.

Box 13   Creating an animal rap

Rap suggestions		Sample rap
Parrot talks	Cow walks	The **blue** whale **sings**
Lion roars	Grandpa snores	And the **hon**ey bee **stings**.
Cat stretches	Dog fetches	The **monk**ey **swings**
Tiger pounces	Kangaroo bounces	When the **tele**phone **rings**.
Bird flies	Baby cries	

Follow-up
For other chants and raps, see Activities 2.7, 4.4, 4.6, 5.1, 5.7, 6.1.

1.12 Animal habitats

Level	* *
Language focus	Simple present tense, *have to, so*
Skills focus	Speaking
Thinking focus	Problem solving
Teaching approach	Promote creativity – accept errors
Interaction	Group work, suitable for large classes
Preparation	Write the sentence stems and the groups of animals on the board. See Box 14.

Procedure

1 Refer the children to the groups of animals on the board.
2 In small groups, ask the children to discuss what would be a suitable habitat for all these animals. Encourage them to use the sentence stems in Box 14.
3 The children will need to think about where the animals can find food and shelter in their habitat.
4 After discussing the possibilities, ask the children to draw an ideal habitat for this combination of animals.

Box 14 Discussing animal habitats

Groups of animals	Sentence stems
Group 1: snake, frog, grasshopper **Group 2:** seagull, worm, fish **Group 3:** brown bear, fish, butterfly	A . . . lives in . . ., so we have to draw . . . A . . . eats . . ., so we have to draw . . . . . . eat . . ., so they have to hide in . . . A . . . sleeps in a . . ., so we have to draw . . .

© Cambridge University Press 2007

Follow-up

Children present their drawings to the class and explain how the habitat is suitable for this group of animals. They could suggest other animals which could share this habitat.

1.13 Animal information report

Level	* * *
Language focus	Information report, simple present tense
Skills focus	Listening for details
Thinking focus	Classifying
Teaching approach	Promote creativity – accept errors
Interaction	Whole class work, suitable for large classes
Preparation	Write the information report headings and questions on the board from Box 15, e.g. *FOOD: What do koalas eat?*

Procedure

1 Explain the meaning of the information report headings to the children.
2 Then choose a sentence at random from the sample information report in Box 15. Read the sentence out to the class.
3 The children have to listen to the sentence and guess which heading matches your sentence. For example, if you read out *Babies are born in summer or spring*, the children should connect this sentence with the *Breeding* heading.

Box 15   Sample information report

Information report: koalas

DEFINITION: What is a koala?
Koalas are native animals from Australia. They are marsupials.

APPEARANCE: What do koalas look like?
The koala is small, grey and furry. They have claws and sharp front teeth.

HABITS: What do koalas do in the daytime / in the night time?
They sleep during the day. They eat for five hours.

BREEDING: Do koalas have a pouch? When are koalas born?
The female koala has a pouch. Babies are born in summer or spring.

LOCATION: Where do koalas live?
Koalas live on the east coast of Australia. They live in eucalyptus forests.

FOOD: What do koalas eat?
Koalas eat eucalyptus leaves. The baby only drinks milk.

PROTECTION: How do koalas protect themselves? Do koalas have enemies?
Koalas use their claws to protect themselves from enemies. Cars, dogs and cats are the koala's enemies.

Follow-up

- The children could write a simple information report about a koala, based on the headings which you have provided.
- The children could research their own animal and write an information report.
- For other information reports, see Activities 1.7, 1.8, 2.8, 2.18, 4.14.

1.14 Human attributes of animals

Level	***
Language focus	Discussion, *because*, *so*, adjectives
Skills focus	Speaking
Thinking focus	Explaining and justifying choices
Teaching approach	Promote creativity – accept errors
Interaction	Group work, suitable for large classes
Preparation	List the animals on the board and write the sentence stems from Box 16. Do not write the personal characteristics.

Procedure

1 Ask the children to suggest a personal characteristic which matches an animal on the board. Write the personal attribute alongside the name of the animal. You may have to give them an example to illustrate. See Box 16. You might also like to add other animals which are familiar to the children.

2 When every animal has a human attribute, ask small groups of children to decide which animals should live in the same community, and give reasons for their choices. For example, *I think the owl and the sheep should live together because the owl is wise and the sheep are stupid. The owl could tell the sheep what to do.* In their discussions, encourage the children to use the sentence stems from the board.

3 Ask the groups to report their findings back to the whole class.

Box 16   Human attributes

Animal	Personal characteristic	Sentence stems
owl	wise, clever	I think . . . and . . .
dog	loyal, friendly	should live together
cat	lazy, clean	because . . .
lion	brave	
pig	dirty	The . . . is . . . , so I
dolphin	playful, intelligent, smart	think it should live
sheep	stupid, silly	with . . .
camel	bad-tempered, unfriendly	
horse	hard-working	The . . . is . . . , so it
elephants	have good memories, hard-working	could not live with . . .
monkeys	talkative, noisy, like to play tricks	
donkeys	hard-working, stubborn	. . . and . . . cannot live
		together because . . .

1.15 Animal advertisements

Level	***
Language focus	Advertisement, adjectives, *must*
Skills focus	Writing
Thinking focus	Considering multiple viewpoints
Teaching approach	Promote creativity – accept errors
Interaction	Individual work, suitable for large classes
Preparation	On a large sheet of paper, draw the sample advertisement from Box 17.

Procedure

1 Ask the children to imagine what would happen if pets were able to advertise for a suitable owner. What kind of person would the pet want? What would the pet expect from its owner?

2 Show the children the sample advertisement from Box 17. Draw their attention to the use of adjectives in the advertisement.

3   Now ask the children to imagine they are a pet. Ask them to design their own advertisement for a pet owner. Pets could be a dog, cat, bird, fish, rabbit or mouse.

Box 17   Advertising for an animal owner

> *WANTED*
> *Clean, warm, quiet home*
> *for a friendly young cat*
> *Owner must supply my favourite food*
> *and*
> *interesting toys*

TIODLES

© Cambridge University Press 2007

Follow-up
Children decorate their advertisements and display them in the classroom.

1.16 Animal conversations

Level	***
Language focus	Conversation, question forms
Skills focus	Speaking
Thinking focus	Imagining
Teaching approach	Promote creativity – accept errors
Interaction	Pairwork, suitable for large classes
Preparation	Write the sentence stems on the board. See Box 18.

Procedure

1 Ask the children to imagine a farm horse. This horse has a relative who is a race horse. The farm horse decides to visit the race horse. What would they say to each other?

2 Ask the children, in pairs, to list some of the questions and topics the animals might talk about. Some topics of conversation, along with some questions, are in Box 18.

3 One partner then takes on the role of a farm horse and the other takes the role of a race horse. They create a conversation between the two animals, using the sentence stems from the board.

Box 18 Horse conversations

Sample conversation	Sentence stems
Farm horse to race horse:	How long do you . . .
Working hours	Do you have . . .
• How long do you have to exercise?	What do you do . . .
• Do you have much leisure time?	Are you . . .
• What do you do during the day?	How fast can you . . .
Attitude of the owner	How many . . . have you . . .
• Are you well cared for?	
Skills	
• How fast can you run?	
• How many races have you won?	
Relationships	
• Are all the other race horses friendly?	

Follow-up

- The children present their dialogues to the class.
- You could do this activity as a writing task. Instead of asking the children to create a dialogue, ask them to write emails which the horses send to each other.
- Other animals that could communicate either by email or in a dialogue include: a pet goldfish and a fish in the ocean; a pet cat and a lion; a farm duck and a wild duck; a farm goat and a mountain goat; a fresh-water fish and a salt-water fish.

1.17 Animal escape

Level	***
Language focus	Recount (radio news item), combination of verb tenses
Skills focus	Listening for facts
Thinking focus	Recognising and selecting
Teaching approach	Promote accuracy – correct errors
Interaction	Individual and pairwork, suitable for large classes
Preparation	Draw the note-taking grid on the board, or make copies for each child. See Box 20. Write the questions and leave the answer section blank.

Procedure

1 Ask the children to copy the note-taking grid from the board. Alternatively, give each child a copy of the note-taking grid. See Box 20.
2 Ask the class to imagine that a crocodile has escaped from the zoo.
3 Ask them what they would hear in the next news flash on the radio. Encourage them to think of a range of information that would be included in a news flash.
4 Read out the news flash from Box 19. Try to use the voice of a radio announcer.
5 While you are reading, the children answer the questions on the grid.
6 Ask the children to check their answers with a partner.
7 Then read the news flash again and the pairs can correct or confirm their answers.

Box 19   Escaped crocodile: news flash

At 10 am today, a large, male crocodile escaped from the zoo. The zoo keeper was entering the cage to feed the animal when he saw it breaking through the fence. Quickly, he phoned the police station to report the escape. If you see the crocodile, you should phone the police on the following number: 180 345 778.

Box 20   Escaped crocodile: note-taking grid

Questions	Children's answers
What escaped from the zoo?	A crocodile
How big is it?	Large
Is it a male or a female?	Male
When did it happen?	At 10 am today
How did it escape?	It broke through the fence
What did the zoo keeper do?	Phoned the police
What is the police phone number?	180 345 778

© Cambridge University Press 2007

Note: A news flash is a recount, but it is factual and objective, unlike the personal recount in Activity 1.10.

Follow-up
For other factual recounts, see Activities 4.16, 5.14.

1.18   Which dog has a better life?

Level	* * *
Language focus	Debate, infinitive, *because*, comparatives
Skills focus	Speaking
Thinking focus	Arguing and justifying
Teaching approach	Promote creativity – accept errors
Interaction	Team work, suitable for large classes
Preparation	Write sentence stems on the board. See Box 21.

Procedure
1   Divide the class into three teams and allocate one of the following working dogs to each team:

- A police dog
- A guide dog (for blind people)
- A farm dog

If other dogs are used in the local community, these could be substituted for any of the above.

2 Either in small groups or in pairs, students discuss why their life is better than the life of the other two dogs. Some suggestions are in Box 21. Encourage the children to use the sentence stems from Box 21.

3 Each team has an opportunity to present their arguments to the class. At the end, they decide which dog has a better life.

Box 21   A dog's life – sample answers

Police dog	Guide dog	Farm dog	Sentence stems
I help the police **to find** missing children or lost people. **I help** the police **to catch** criminals. **I save time for** the busy policemen **because I can** smell.	**I help** blind people to shop, and **to catch** buses and trains. **I am** a friend to a disabled person. **I save money for** blind people **because I can** help them walk.	**I am** the farmer's best friend. **I help** the farmer **to round up** sheep or cows. **I save money for** the farmer **because I do not** need petrol.	I am . . . I help . . . to . . . I save time for . . . because . . . I save money for . . . because I can/do not . . .

Follow-up

- Ask the class to describe the personal attributes these working dogs have in common. Suggestions are in Box 22.
- For another debate, see Activity 2.17.

Box 22   Attributes of working dogs

These working dogs are: loyal, trustworthy, hard-working, clever, quick learners, strong, they serve the community.

---

2 Journeys

2.1 A beach holiday

Level	*
Language focus	Common nouns: kinship terms, simple present tense
Skills focus	Pronunciation: consonant sounds
Thinking focus	Giving a reason for a choice
Teaching approach	Promote accuracy – correct errors
Interaction	Whole class work, suitable for large classes, pairwork
Preparation	Write the sentence stems on the board. See Box 24.

Procedure

1 Ask the children to recall all the people they know and then list the vocabulary on the board. Suggestions are contained in Box 23. Some children may suggest the given name of a brother, sister or friend. Acknowledge the response, and then ask for more information about the person, e.g. *Katherine . . . Yes . . . And Katherine is your . . . friend/sister/baby sister/big sister?*

2 Then say *Imagine you are going on a beach holiday. Choose eight of these people to come with you.* The children write their lists of people.

3 Ask the children to think about why they are choosing these eight people.

4 Refer to the sentence stems on the board, and ask the children to share their list with a partner and give reasons for their choices. Some examples of answers are in Box 24.

5 Draw the children's attention to the final *s* sound when using contractions, possessives or third person, and for internal consonant sounds, e.g. *brother, baby, sister.*

Box 23   Holiday company

mum/mother, dad/father, brother, big brother, little brother, baby brother, sister, big sister, little sister, baby sister, grandfather/grandpa, grandmother/grandma, friend, best friend, good friend, sister's friend, brother's friend

---

Box 24   Why are they coming?

Who do you choose?	+ Because	Why do you choose this person?	Sentence stems
I choose Emma. I choose my baby brother. I choose my dad. I choose Jack. I choose my brother. I choose Ben. I choose my grandpa. I choose my grandma. I choose my mother. I choose Anna. I choose the dog.		She is my friend. He likes water. He can drive the car. He plays the guitar. He can play football. He's Jack's friend. He's got a fishing rod. She likes the view. She likes holidays. She's got a little TV. She likes the sand.	I choose . . . because he/she is . . . he/she can . . . he/she plays . . . he/she likes . . . he/she has got . . .

2.2 Describing what we can do on a beach holiday

Level	*
Language focus	*Can*
Skills focus	Speaking and writing
Thinking focus	Listing and recalling
Teaching approach	Promote accuracy – correct errors
Interaction	Whole class work, suitable for large classes
Preparation	Prepare a wallchart with headings. See Box 25. Cut up blank cards to attach to the wallchart.

Procedure

1 Ask the children to name something they would like to take on a beach holiday to give them something to do while they are away, e.g. *A ball.*

2 When a child responds, another child is appointed to ask *If you take a ball, what can you do?*

3 The first child could respond *I can catch a ball. / I can kick a ball. / I can throw a ball. / I can play football.* Suggestions of other items are in Box 25.

4 Children may want to express their own ideas, but they may not have the vocabulary to do so. For example, they may want to take a pack of playing cards, or a computer game. You can either provide the vocabulary or encourage the children to use a bilingual dictionary.

5 On a card, children write the items they would like to take on the holiday. On another card, they write what they can do. They then attach their cards to a class chart, similar to Box 25. They may like to include their name on the card, e.g. *Kate will take coloured pens. Kate can draw pictures.*

Box 25   Holiday activities

What will you take?	What can you do?
coloured pens	draw pictures
books	read stories
bicycle	ride a bicycle
radio	listen to music
basketball	play basketball
fishing rod	catch fish
guitar	play/sing songs
camera	take photos

2.3 Types of transport

Level	*
Language focus	Vocabulary: transport
Skills focus	Speaking and writing
Thinking focus	Classifying
Teaching approach	Promote accuracy – correct errors
Interaction	Team work and pairwork, suitable for large classes

Procedure

1 Divide the children into two teams. Each team takes a turn to suggest a form of transport. The game continues until all possibilities have been exhausted. You may have to supply a word when children describe a form of transport, but do not have the vocabulary, e.g. *a sailing boat, a ferry.*

2 List these forms of transport randomly on the board.
3 Then ask the children to draw a table with three columns and, in pairs, write the transport under the categories, e.g. sea, air and land transport. See Box 26.
4 Call on pairs to read out their answers.

Box 26   Classifying transport

Sea	Air	Land
boat	helicopter	car
sailing boat	plane	train
ferry	space ship	bus
ship	hot air balloon	motorbike
canoe	jet	lorry

2.4 Transport: odd one out

Level	*
Language focus	Vocabulary: transport, *but*
Skills focus	Listening, writing
Thinking focus	Differentiating
Teaching approach	Promote creativity – accept errors
Interaction	Pairwork, suitable for large classes

1 Read out four transport words from Box 27. This is a simple dictation.
2 The children write the words.
3 In pairs, the children try to find the 'odd one out'. When they think they have found it, they should give a reason for their choice, using *but* to signal the odd one out. See Box 27 for some examples.

Note: In this activity, there could be more than one correct answer, e.g. in the first example, *bike* could be chosen, because only one person usually rides a bike and more than one person travels in the other means of transport. Alternatively, *bike* could be chosen because you ride *in* a car, helicopter and plane, but you ride *on* a bike. Provided a feasible reason is given, the answer should be counted as correct.

Box 27   Transport vocabulary

List of four words	Odd one out	Reason
car, bike, helicopter, plane	plane	A small number of people can travel in cars, in helicopters and on bikes, but a large number of people can travel in a plane.
boat, motorbike, train, car	boat	A boat travels on water, but the others travel on land.
boat, plane, lorry, bus	lorry	Boats, planes and buses carry passengers, but a lorry carries goods.
bike, motorbike, bus, train	train	Bikes, motorbikes and buses travel on the road, but a train travels on tracks.

Follow-up

To extend this activity, ask the children to use their dictionaries to create their own transport word challenge for their classmates.

2.5 A travel sociogram

Level	*
Language focus	Language of location
Skills focus	Speaking
Thinking focus	Giving reasons
Teaching approach	Promote creativity – accept errors
Interaction	Pairwork: information gap, suitable for large classes
Preparation	Photocopy the sociogram from Box 28. Make two copies for each child.

Procedure

1 Tell the class that some people are going on a holiday together in a car.
2 Give out the photocopied sociograms and tell the children that the car has three rows of seats: two people can sit in the front, three can sit in the middle row, and three can sit in the back row.

Box 28   Car sociogram

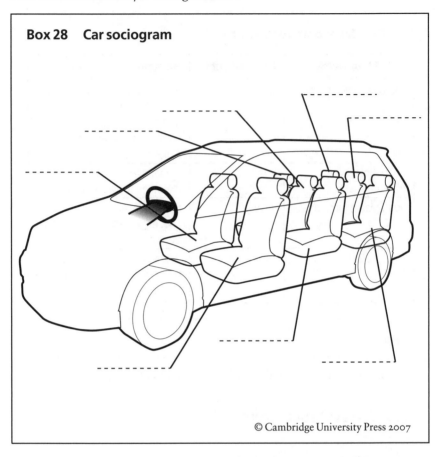

© Cambridge University Press 2007

3 Ask the children to decide who is in the car and where everyone should sit. They write the names of the people on the lines. They could include people from Box 23.

4 Encourage the children to think about why these people are placed in these seats.

5 On the board, write some expressions of location, e.g. *next to, behind, between, in front of*.

6 Now one child gives directions to his/her partner, who has to listen and try to copy the seating plan, without looking at it. When one partner has completed the task, the other has a turn to give his/her seating plan.

7 When they have finished, the partners check their answers.

Box 29   Seating plan

Seating plan in the car	+ Because	Reason for placement
Mum can sit in the front. Dad can sit next to Mum. Grandma and Grandpa can sit behind Jack and me. My sister can sit next to Grandma. Jack can sit between me and Ben. I can sit behind Mum.		Mum can drive the car. Dad can read the map. They can sleep. She can look out of the window. He can talk to us. I can sing to Mum.

Follow-up

In pairs, children have to give reasons for their seating plans. Suggestions for these are in Box 29.

2.6 A beach holiday checklist

Level	*
Language focus	Checklist, numbers *one* to *ten*, vocabulary: clothing and hobbies
Skills focus	Spelling
Thinking focus	Ranking and judging
Teaching approach	Promote accuracy – correct errors
Interaction	Individual work, suitable for large classes

Procedure

1 Ask the children to write the numbers *one* to *ten* (in words) down the left-hand margin of the page. Check their spelling.

2 The children then create a holiday checklist for themselves. They write the things that they have to remember to take away on a beach holiday. The catch is that you would not take ten hats, so the children have to come up with a feasible list. See Box 30 for suggestions.

Box 30   Beach holiday checklist

one	hat
two	pairs of shoes
three	shirts
four	pairs of trousers
five	pairs of socks
six	T-shirts
seven	books
eight	badminton shuttlecocks
nine	fish hooks
ten	coloured pencils

Follow-up

Ask the children to draw up a checklist for another sort of holiday, e.g. a holiday in the snow, hiking in a forest, climbing a mountain, or visiting a famous city.

2.7 Travelling to school

Level	**
Language focus	Chant, *who*, simple present tense
Skills focus	Pronunciation: stress, rhythm, final sounds
Thinking focus	Recalling
Teaching approach	Promote accuracy – correct errors
Interaction	Whole class chant, suitable for large classes

Procedure

1   Ask the question *Who walks to school?*
2   Choose one child to answer *I walk to school.*
3   The class then chants ***Sam** is the **boy** who **walks** to **school**.* (The stressed words are in bold.)
4   Draw the class's attention to the final *s* sound in *walks*.
5   Repeat the question *Who walks to school?*

6   The chant will build up to include a few more children who walk to school, e.g. *Sam is the boy who **walks** to school; Mary is the girl who **walks** to school.*

7   Then change the question: *Who rides to school?*

8   The children's responses continue to add to the chant, e.g. *Sam is the boy who **walks** to school; Mary is the girl who **walks** to school; Ben is the boy who **rides** to school.* Encourage a singsong type of chanting.

9   Further questions and answers are in Box 31.

Box 31   Transport chant

Q: Who comes to school by car?
A: **Josh** is the **boy** who **comes** by **car**.
Q: Who catches the bus?
A: **Lisa** is the **girl** who **catches** the **bus**.
Q: Who takes the train?
A: **Ann** is the **girl** who **takes** the **train**.

Follow-up

•   The children construct a graph showing how many walk, ride, catch a bus, or catch a train to school. They can then report either in writing or orally, e.g. *Six children walk to school; nine children catch the bus.*

•   For other chants and raps, see Activities 1.11, 4.4, 4.6, 5.1, 5.7, 6.1.

2.8 About the weather

Level	* *
Language focus	Information report, definition, simple present tense
Skills focus	Writing
Thinking focus	Creating
Teaching approach	Promote creativity – accept errors
Interaction	Group work, suitable for large classes
Preparation	You need seven large sheets of paper. Write one question on the top of each large sheet of paper. See Box 32.

Procedure

1   Divide the class into seven groups and give each group a sheet of paper containing a question about an element of the weather, e.g. *What is a rainbow?* See Box 32 for other questions and a sample answer.

2   The group has one minute to decide on a response and write it on the piece of paper.
3   The pieces of paper are then rotated to another group.
4   The children read the question and the answers of their peers. They decide on another bullet point they can add to the response. Some teachers may prefer that the learners use scientific knowledge, while other teachers may encourage some creative thinking, e.g. *When the giants in the sky move their furniture, it makes thunder.*
5   Continue to rotate the pieces of paper until every group has contributed or until they run out of time or ideas.

Box 32   Weather questions

	Example: What is a rainbow?
1 What is a rainbow? **2** What is rain? **3** What is snow? **4** What is a cloud? **5** What is thunder? **6** What is lightning? **7** What is wind?	• A rainbow is an arch/arc/bow/semi-circle in the sky. • It has seven colours. • The colours are red, orange, yellow, green, blue, indigo and violet. • A rainbow comes/appears after the rain. • A rainbow has/contains/is made up of water droplets. • Light shines through a rainbow. • Some people say a rainbow means good luck.

Follow-up
•   The children illustrate their original sheet of paper and display their work on the classroom wall.
•   For other information reports, see Activities 1.7, 1.8, 1.13, 2.18, 4.14.

2.9 Advice for a visitor

Level	* *
Language focus	Procedure, imperatives
Skills focus	Reading
Thinking focus	Sequencing
Teaching approach	Promote accuracy – correct errors
Interaction	Pairwork, suitable for large classes
Preparation	Copy the procedure from Box 33, but jumble the order of the instructions. Alternatively, you could copy the procedure and cut it up into individual instructions.

Procedure

1 Tell the class that they are going to prepare some advice for a visitor. This advice will help the visitor to use public transport in your area.

2 This activity can be done in two ways. You could give the children a jumbled version of the procedure in Box 33 and ask them, in pairs, to sort the procedure into the correct order. Alternatively, you could cut up the procedure into separate sentence strips and ask the pairs to put the instructions into the correct order. Encourage the children to look for the sequencing language to help them decide on the order of instructions.

3 When the instructions are in the correct order, ask the children to number them *1–7* and check their answers.

Note: You may want to change some of the instructions, so that they match your local situation.

Box 33   Catching a train

Procedure: How to catch a train

- Go to the ticket machine.
- First, choose either a single or return ticket.
- Then choose either an adult or a child ticket.
- After you have chosen the type of ticket you want, enter information about where you are going.
- The machine will show you the price of the ticket.
- Then put your money into the machine.
- Take your ticket out of the machine.

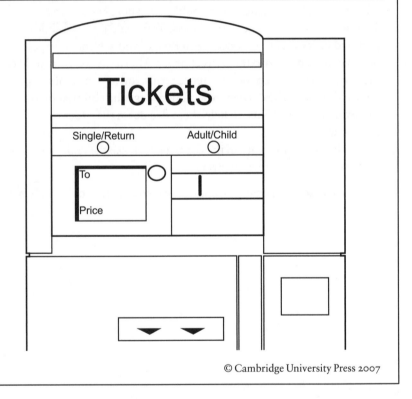

© Cambridge University Press 2007

Follow-up

For other procedures, see Activities 3.4, 4.12, 4.15, 4.18, 5.8, 6.10, 6.13, 6.16.

2.10 How do you come to school?

Level	**
Language focus	*but, because*
Skills focus	Listening and speaking
Thinking focus	Distinguishing between contrast and reason
Teaching approach	Promote accuracy – correct errors
Interaction	Whole class activity, suitable for large classes

Procedure

1 Read out a sentence stem from Box 34.
2 Choose one child to complete the sentence with *but*.
3 Then choose another child to complete the same sentence with *because*.
4 The sentences could describe how the children really come to school, or they could be fun and imaginative, e.g. *on a donkey*.

Box 34   Coming to school

Sentence stem pattern 1	Sentence stem pattern 2	Fun ideas
I always catch a bus to school, but . . . because . . . I never take a train to school, but . . . because . . . I sometimes ride a bike to school, but . . . because . . .	Usually I come to school by car, but . . . because . . . Often I come to school on foot, but . . . because . . . Occasionally I come to school on a motorbike, but . . . because . . .	Sometimes I run to school, but . . . because . . . Usually I swim to school, but . . . because . . . Occasionally I fly to school, but . . . because . . . Sometimes I skate to school, but . . . because . . . Often I come to school by helicopter / jet / space ship, but . . . because . . .

Follow-up

Ask the children to write their own sentence stems and read them out to their classmates. They then choose a classmate to complete the sentence stem with *but* or *because*.

2.11 Guess the local place

Level	**
Language focus	Description, simple present tense
Skills focus	Writing
Thinking focus	Selecting and evaluating
Teaching approach	Promote creativity – accept errors
Interaction	Team work, suitable for large classes

Procedure

1 Divide the class into teams. Then set the children a challenge. They have to write three clues about a local building or place of interest. The trick is to write ambiguous clues, so that the answer is not immediately obvious, or could refer to more than one place. See Box 35 for examples.

2 Team members take turns to read out a clue. If a rival team makes an incorrect guess, they are out of the game. If they guess the place after one clue, they score three points; after two clues, they score two points; and after three clues, they score one point. If no other team can guess the place, then the writers of the clues score three points.

Box 35   Community locations

Place	Clues
Library	**(1)** It has many shelves. **(2)** Lots of people visit here. **(3)** It is usually very quiet.
Hospital	**(1)** It is a large building. **(2)** It is always open. **(3)** Many people sleep here.
Zoo	**(1)** It has some buildings and some open spaces. **(2)** Children love to visit here. **(3)** You have to pay to enter.

2.12 Writing a 'late note' for the teacher

Level	* *
Language focus	Letter, simple past tense
Skills focus	Writing
Thinking focus	Explaining
Teaching approach	Promote creativity – accept errors
Interaction	Individual work, suitable for large classes
Preparation	You may have to provide a general outline of a letter format showing where to write the address, date, greeting and closing comments. Most student text books have a standard letter format, or you may have a particular format you prefer.

Procedure

1　This activity can be done in a few ways. It could be used to reflect real situations when children are late for class. Alternatively, you could encourage the children to make up unbelievable excuses. See Box 36 for suggestions. Another possibility is to set limitations on the excuse, e.g. *It must have something to do with the weather.*

2　Ask the children to think about why they could be late for class. Their excuses are listed on the board.

3　Then ask the children to write a short 'late note', giving a reason why they may have been late for class. This should be limited to one or two sentences.

4　Select children to read out their late notes.

Box 36　Excuses

The wind blew my hat away.
The snow blocked our driveway.
The rain wet my homework.
The train was late.
The bus broke down.
An elephant sat on our car.
A crocodile ate my school bag.
Our helicopter ran out of petrol.

Follow-up

• Some teachers regularly use 'late notes' to create an authentic purpose for writing.

• For other letters, cards and emails, see Activities 4.8, 5.11, 5.15, 6.8.

2.13 Travel diary from space

Level	* * *
Language focus	Personal recount, question forms, simple past tense
Skills focus	Speaking
Thinking focus	Imagining and creating
Teaching approach	Promote creativity – accept errors
Interaction	Turn-taking around the class, suitable for large classes
Preparation	Write the questions on the board. See Box 37.

Procedure

1   Explain to the class that they are going to create an oral travel diary about a journey to an imaginary planet. Encourage the children to be creative when giving their answers.
2   Choose one child to ask the first question: *Where did you go?*
3   This child then chooses a classmate to answer the question. The child who answers then chooses another student to ask the next question, selecting from the questions on the board.
4   This pattern continues until all the questions have been asked.
5   By this stage, the children may be able to invent their own questions.

Box 37   Questions about space travel

Questions	Possible student answers
Where did you go?	I went to the purple planet.
How long did it take?	It took five minutes.
How much did it cost?	It cost one hundred pounds.
What did you eat?	I ate purple ice cream.
What did it taste like?	It was sweet.
What did it smell like?	It smelt like grapes.

Follow-up
For other personal recounts, see Activities 1.10, 2.15, 4.17.

2.14 Singing about journeys

Level	* * *
Language focus	Song, present perfect tense
Skills focus	Writing: joint construction, Pronunciation: stress
Thinking focus	Creating
Teaching approach	Promote accuracy – correct errors
Interaction	Whole class, suitable for large classes
Preparation	Become familiar with the melody of the song.
	Write sentence stems and clues on the board. See Box 38.

Procedure

1 Introduce the melody of the song *Galway Bay*. Check the Appendix for a website link to this melody. See page 148.
2 Using the sentence stems and clues on the board, ask the children to help you construct a song about travelling to Saturn. See Box 38.
3 The children sing the song together, making sure they stress the syllables in bold.

Box 38   Travelling to Saturn

Sentence stems	Clues
Have you **ever** . . . **across** the sky to **Sat**urn,	gazed / looked / stared
And **seen** . . . spin round in **space**?	
Have you **ever** watched . . . at **night** time,	What would you see on Saturn?
And wished that you could **trav**el to this	What could you see at
place?	night time?

Box 39 Example songs

1 Saturn

Have you ever gazed across the sky to Saturn,
And seen the golden rings spin round in space?
Have you ever watched its icy moons at night time,
And wished that you could travel to this place?

2 Sydney

Have you ever sailed around the world to Sydney,
And seen the opera house and harbour bridge?
Have you ever ridden in a harbour ferry,
Or swum among the waves at Bondi Beach?

3 China

Have you ever sailed around the world to China,
And walked along the great wall in your boots?
Have you ever eaten rice and meat with chopsticks,
Or fed a panda bear with bamboo shoots?

Follow-up

- In groups, the children create other songs about places they would like to visit, and perform these songs to the class. Some examples are in Box 39.
- For other songs, see Activities 1.5, 5.4, 6.7.

2.15 UFO

Level	* * *
Language focus	Personal recount, simple past tense, past continuous
Skills focus	Listening and speaking
Thinking focus	Paraphrasing and retelling
Teaching approach	Promote creativity – accept errors
Interaction	Group work or pairs, suitable for large classes

Procedure

1 Tell the children that they are going to do a mini dictogloss activity.
2 Read the personal recount aloud at normal speed. See Box 40.
3 The children listen for the gist of the text, but do not write at this stage.
4 Read the text at normal speed again.

5   This time, the children write down key vocabulary while you are reading. These words are usually nouns, adjectives, adverbs and action verbs rather than words like the verb *to be*, pronouns or prepositions.

6   In small groups, the children reconstruct the original text. Note that this is **not** a dictation. The aim of the activity is to create a text which paraphrases the meaning of the original text, so children may use synonyms, or may omit parts of the text which are not particularly pertinent to the overall gist.

Box 40   An alien took my dog!

I was walking my dog, Pluto, last night when I saw a strange light in the sky. I wondered if it could be a UFO. Then I saw it! It was a large flying saucer. Suddenly, an alien appeared at the door. I ran away, but where was Pluto? My poor dog had disappeared!

Follow-up

*   Display the children's reconstructions in the classroom, along with the teacher's original text. These could be accompanied by their illustrations.
*   For other personal recounts, see Activities 1.10, 2.13, 4.17.
*   For further information about dictogloss, see:
    Cameron, L. 2001:119 *Teaching Languages to Young Learners* Cambridge: Cambridge University Press.
    Wajnrb, R. 1990 *Grammar Dictation* Oxford: Oxford University Press.

2.16 Science fiction

Level	* * *
Language focus	Narrative
Skills focus	Speaking
Thinking focus	Imagining and creating
Teaching approach	Promote creativity – accept errors
Interaction	Group work, suitable for large classes

Procedure

1   Divide the class into three groups.

2   The first group has to think about the **characters** that could appear in a science fiction story.

3   The second group has to think about different **settings** for a science fiction story.
4   The third group has to think about a possible **plot** for a science fiction story.
5   Then reform the groups, so that each new group consists of an expert on characters, an expert on setting and an expert on plot. The new group members share their ideas. This is called a jigsaw activity.

Box 41   Story plan

Characters	you, your friend, aliens, space creatures, monsters, astronauts
Setting	planet, future time, past time, jungle, desert, cave
Plot	lost in space; captured by an alien; visited by a UFO; travel backwards/forwards in time; discover a new planet

---

Follow-up
• The children record their story plan on a grid. See Box 41.
• Each group writes their cooperative story and illustrates it. Stories are displayed on the walls of the classroom.
• For other narratives, see Activities 3.5, 3.13, 3.14, 3.18, 4.10, 5.1, 6.18.

2.17   Holidays in space

Level	***
Language focus	Debate, modal expressions
Skills focus	Speaking
Thinking focus	Analysing, contrasting and evaluating
Teaching approach	Promote creativity – accept errors
Interaction	Whole class, suitable for large classes
	Group discussion
Preparation	Draw a large grid on the board. See Box 42.

Procedure
1   Write the topic on the board: *Holidays in space*.
2   Refer to the large grid on the board.
3   Tell the children that you want them to think of the advantages and disadvantages of having a holiday in space. Give them an example of the sort of ideas that can appear in each section of the grid. See Box 43 for suggestions.

4 Divide the class into teams, and each team has a turn to add one idea to the strengths and weaknesses grid. Team members discuss their answers first and then choose one idea to add to the grid. Encourage the children to use the modal expressions *could/couldn't, might, would* and *may*. They continue until they run out of ideas.

5 The team to contribute the last idea is the winner.

Box 42   Space travel: strengths and weaknesses grid

Topic: Holidays in space	
Strengths	**Weaknesses**

Box 43   Questions about space travel

Strengths

Teacher: What are the good things about going on a holiday into space? What would we enjoy? How would we benefit?

Children: It's a new experience. We could see things we've never seen before, e.g. Saturn's rings, Mars' volcano. We could see the Earth from space. We might meet other friendly life forms. We might learn about how the solar system was formed.

Weaknesses

Teacher: What are some of the problems we could face? What would stop us from going on a holiday in space?

Children: It's too expensive. We would be away for a long time. We couldn't eat our normal food. It's too hot / too cold. There could be angry aliens in space. The space ship may break down.

Follow-up

• You could use the grid as a springboard for writing paragraphs in favour of and against holidaying in space.

• For other debates, see Activity 1.18.

2.18 About Mars

Level	* * *
Language focus	Information report, simple present tense
Skills focus	Listening for key words, spelling
Thinking focus	Grouping information
Teaching approach	Promote accuracy – correct errors
Interaction	Whole class, suitable for large classes
Preparation	Photocopy the note-taking grid from Box 44. Do not copy the answers.

Procedure

1   Give the children a copy of the note-taking grid. See Box 44.
    Note: Some answers are given in the answer grid, so that the children
    know what kind of information to put there. You may need to explain
    this vocabulary before you read.

2   Tell the children that you are going to read some information about Mars
    and they have to listen and complete the grid.

3   Read out the information about Mars at a slow and steady pace. See Box
    45. This is not a dictation, so your speed of delivery should be a little
    faster than for dictation. The children are listening for key words in order
    to take notes.

4   When you have finished reading, ask the children to check their answers
    with a partner.

Follow-up

• You could ask the children to write a paragraph about Mars, using their
  notes.

• You may prefer to do this activity as a reading task. You could photocopy
  the text in Box 45 and ask the children to take notes from the text, using
  the note-taking grid in Box 44.

• For other information reports, see Activities 1.7, 1.8, 1.13, 2.8, 4.14.

Box 44   Mars: note-taking grid

Note-taking questions	Note-taking answer grid	Note-taking answers
Where is Mars? Made out of . . . ? Temperature? Colour? Some features of Mars? Life on Mars? Water on Mars?	Craters, volcanoes	Closest to Earth Rock Cold Red Ice caps, craters, deep valleys, volcanoes Not found / Don't know yet / Scientists looking Not found / Don't know yet / Scientists looking

© Cambridge University Press 2007

Box 45   Mars: information report

Mars is the closest planet to Earth. It is made out of rock. It is very cold and has ice caps, just like the North and South Poles on Earth. From the Earth, Mars looks red. Mars has many craters, some deep valleys and some tall volcanoes. Some scientists say that there might be life on Mars, but they haven't found any life yet. Scientists are also looking for water on Mars.

Fantasy and adventure

3.1 The king and the dragon

Level	*
Language focus	Description, simple present tense, prepositions of place
Skills focus	Listening for details
Thinking focus	Recalling
Teaching approach	Promote accuracy – correct errors
Interaction	Whole class work, suitable for large classes

Procedure

1   On the board, write the key vocabulary for this activity: *dragon, tree, king*.
2   Check that the children know the meaning of these words and how they are pronounced.
3   Now tell the class that you are going to read a small description. You would like them to draw the picture as you read.
4   Read the dragon description from Box 46 and pause after each sentence for the children to draw what they hear.
5   Check that the children have accurately represented the events of the description.
6   Ask the children to share their pictures with their classmates.

Follow-up

Ask the children to write the dragon description in their own words under their illustration.

Box 46   Dragon description

There is a dragon which lives **in** a tree. Every day a king sits **under** the dragon's tree. He reads stories to the dragon.

© Cambridge University Press 2007

3.2 The pirate

Level	*
Language focus	Description, simple present tense
Skills focus	Reading for meaning
Thinking focus	Inferring
Teaching approach	Promote accuracy – correct errors
Interaction	Whole class work, suitable for large classes
Preparation	Either write the cloze activity on the board or copy it onto a transparency. See Box 47.

Procedure

1 Ask the children to tell you what they know about pirates. For example, *Where do they live? What do they wear? What do they look like?*
2 Explain to the class that you have written a small description of a pirate, but some words are missing from each sentence.
3 Ask the children to choose the correct word from under the description and help you to complete the sentences. Encourage discussion in the class as the children decide on their answers.
4 Write the answers in the gaps in the cloze activity.

Box 47   Description of a pirate

Cloze activity	Answers
I **(1)** . . . on a boat.	1 I live on a boat.
I **(2)** . . . fish every day.	2 I eat fish every day.
I **(3)** . . . on a wooden leg.	3 I walk on a wooden leg.
I **(4)** . . . a black hat.	4 I wear a black hat.
I **(5)** . . . to my parrot.	5 I talk to my parrot.
eat talk wear live walk	

Note: In this reading activity, the children may not know the meaning of *wooden*, but they would know the word *leg*. Ask them to guess what kind of leg the pirate might have. Alternatively, break the word into *wood – en*. They may know the word *wood* and can guess the meaning from there.

3.3 Adventurers and heroes

Level	*
Language focus	Proper nouns
Skills focus	Pronunciation: stressed and unstressed syllables
Thinking focus	Matching
Teaching approach	Promote accuracy – correct errors
Interaction	Whole class work, suitable for large classes
Preparation	Write a list of heroes and adventurers on the board. Choose from the learners' column of Box 48. Either select names which are familiar to the children, or take the opportunity to introduce some heroes from other cultures. Make sure you mix up the patterns and write them randomly on the board, i.e. don't write all the same patterns together.

Procedure

1 Write the name of one adventurer or hero on the board. Choose from the teacher's column in Box 48. Clap out the rhythm of the name, paying attention to stressed and unstressed syllables. Say the name as you clap. (The national origin of names are included in this activity for added interest.)

2 Ask the children to clap and copy as they say the word you have chosen.

3 Next, ask the children to find a similar pattern from the list on the board. See the learners' column in Box 48.

4 Then ask the children to clap out the two names, one after the other, and say the names as they clap, e.g. *Superman, Monkey King.*

5 Encourage the children to find other words with a similar pattern and add these to the chanting and clapping, e.g. *Superman, Monkey King, Samurai.*

6 Next, choose another word from the teacher's column. Clap the rhythm as you say the word.

7 Ask the children to find a word with a similar pattern.

8 Clap out the two names as you say them together, e.g. *Batman, Frog Prince.*

9 Continue until all the words in the teacher's column have been used. (Talk about the national origin for added interest.)

Box 48   Chanting heroes' names

Teacher's column	Learners' column
Superman: **Su** – per – man (USA)	Spiderman: **Spi** – der – man (USA) Pokemon: **Pok** – e – mon (Japan) Emperor: **Em** – per – or (Japan, China) Samurai: **Sam** – ur – ai (Japan) Monkey King: **Mon** – key – King (China) Robin Hood: **Rob** – in – Hood (England)
Catwoman: **Cat** – wom – an (USA)	Snake Charmer: **Snake** – Charm – er (India)
Batman: **Bat** – **man** (USA)	Frog Prince: **Frog** – **Prince** (Germany)
Harry Potter: **Har** – ry **Pott** – er (UK)	Kung Fu Master: **Kung** – Fu – **Ma** – ster (China)

3.4 Witch's magic potion

Level	*
Language focus	Procedure, possessives
Skills focus	Writing
Thinking focus	Inventing
Teaching approach	Promote creativity – accept errors
Interaction	Pairwork, suitable for large classes
Preparation	Write the animals from Box 49 on the board.

Procedure

1 Tell the children that they are going to invent a witch's magic potion.

2 Ask the children to write down the five animals from the board.

3 Show them how to use the possessive apostrophe + *s* after the name of each animal, e.g. *bird's.*

4 Then ask them, in pairs, to choose something from that animal that they could use in a witch's magic potion. They may have to use bilingual dictionaries to find the exact word they want to use.

5 The children then write the witch's magic potion. A model is in Box 50.

Box 49   Animals and ingredients

Animal	Possible ingredients
A bird	feather, nest, egg
A cat	whisker, hair, purr, claw
A fish	scale, fin, egg
A snake	tooth, fang, scale, hiss, poison
A spider	web, egg, poison

Box 50   Model: witch's potion

1 bird's feather
1 cat's whisker
1 fish's scale
1 snake's tooth
1 spider's egg

Follow-up

- The children illustrate and display their magic potions.
- The children could develop this list of ingredients into a recipe. They could write the instructions for mixing and heating the ingredients.
- By choosing animals and ingredients which start with the same letter, e.g. *cat's claw, fish's fin*, you could create a class chant. You could also write some of the ingredients in the plural form, e.g. *five fish fins*.
- For other procedures, see Activities 2.9, 4.12, 4.15, 4.18, 5.8, 6.10, 6.13, 6.16.

3.5 Good king bad king

Level	*
Language focus	Narrative, antonyms, simple present tense
Skills focus	Listening and speaking
Thinking focus	Contrasting
Teaching approach	Promote creativity – accept errors
Interaction	Whole class work, suitable for large classes

Procedure

1   Begin by starting to tell the story. Use a very expressive voice: *In a faraway place there lives a good king.* See Box 51.

2   Tell the children that when you emphasise a word, they have to suggest an opposite word. They should say *In a faraway place there lives a bad king.* If children are more familiar with the term *Emperor*, then use this instead of *King*.

3   Continue telling the story, emphasising the words in bold and asking the children to suggest an opposite, or something that has a negative message. See Box 51 for some suggestions.

Box 51   Good king story

Good king	Bad king
In a faraway place there lives a **good** king.	bad
He is very **young** and **handsome**.	old and ugly
He wears **beautiful, clean, new** clothes.	ugly, dirty, old
For breakfast he eats **eggs**.	snakes
For lunch he eats **bananas**.	horse hair
For supper he eats **rice**.	children
All day he drinks **orange juice**.	onion juice

Follow-up

- The children write the description of the bad king. They illustrate their description and display it in the classroom.
- For other narratives, see Activities 2.16, 3.13, 3.14, 3.18, 4.10, 5.1, 6.18.

3.6 Draw a dinosaur

Level	*
Language focus	Description, vocabulary: body parts, numbers, colours
Skills focus	Listening for details
Thinking focus	Recalling
Teaching approach	Promote accuracy – correct errors
Interaction	Whole class work, suitable for large classes

Procedure

1 Ask the class to take out coloured pencils and paper. Tell them they are going to draw a mystery animal.

2 Explain to the children that the drawing is a side-on view of the animal, and demonstrate this by standing side-on to the class, e.g. they will see only one eye.

3 Carefully read out the description of the mystery animal from Box 52, one line at a time.

4 When you have finished, check the children's drawings to see that they have followed your instructions. Ask them to guess what they have drawn. They should have something resembling a Tyrannosaurus Rex.

Follow-up

Ask the children to prepare their own descriptions of a mystery animal. Ask them, in pairs, to describe their animal for their partner to draw. They should then check that their partner has understood their instructions.

Box 52   Description of a mystery animal

Draw a large green body in the shape of an egg.
Draw a short thick green neck.
Draw a green head in the shape of an egg.
Draw one black eye.
Draw a big red mouth with lots of sharp teeth.
Draw a big green tail like a crocodile's tail.
Draw two thick green legs like the legs of an elephant.
Draw two little green arms.

© Cambridge University Press 2007

3.7 Wizard interview

Level	**
Language focus	Interview, question forms, adverbs of frequency, simple present tense
Skills focus	Speaking
Thinking focus	Inventing
Teaching approach	Promote creativity – accept errors
Interaction	Pairwork, suitable for large classes
Preparation	Write the interview questions on the board, along with adverbs of frequency from Box 53.

Procedure

1 Put the children into pairs. Tell them that one person will be the interviewer and the other person will be a wizard. If they are not familiar with *wizard*, choose another magical person like a fairy or a witch.

2 One person in the pair asks the questions and the other has to imagine and invent a response. Questions and some possible answers are in Box 53.

3 When they have finished asking and answering questions, call on the person asking the questions to talk to the class about the wizard he/she interviewed. See Box 53 for a sample answer.

Box 53   Wizard interview grid

Interview questions	Wizard answers	Sample answer
Where do you live?	I live in a tree in the forest.	Sam is a wizard and he lives in a tree in a forest.
How often do you make magic spells?	I **sometimes** make magic spells.	He sometimes makes magic spells.
When do you make magic spells?	I **usually** make magic spells in the evening.	He usually makes magic spells in the evening.
How do you make magic spells?	I use a bowl and mix up grass and leaves from the forest. I **usually** say magic words when I am mixing.	He mixes grass and leaves and says magic words when he is mixing.

3.8 Turned into a rabbit!

Level	**
Language focus	Personal description, simple present tense
Skills focus	Writing
Thinking focus	Imagining
Teaching approach	Promote creativity – accept errors
Interaction	Individual work, suitable for large classes
Preparation	Write headings and prompt questions on the board. See Box 54.

Procedure

1 Tell the class to imagine that a wicked witch has turned them all into rabbits. Ask them to think about how their life is different now.
2 Refer to the headings and prompt questions that you have written on the board. Ask the children to consider these factors when thinking about how their lives have changed.
3 Ask the children to write a short paragraph describing their life as a rabbit. They should use the question prompts to help them. Some possible answers are in Box 54.

Box 54   My life as a rabbit

	Appearance	Home	Size	Clothes	Food	School
Prompt questions	What do you look like?	Where do you live?	How big are you?	What do you wear?	What do you eat?	Where do you go to school?
Possible answers	I am furry and I have very large ears.	I live in a hole in the ground.	I am small.	I do not wear clothes. I have fur.	I eat carrots and lettuce.	I do not have to go to school!

Follow-up
Choose other animals that could be the result of a wicked witch's spell, e.g. you have been turned into a frog, a cat or a mouse.

3.9 Queen's family

Level	**
Language focus	Vocabulary: kinship terms
Skills focus	Listening for details
Thinking focus	Following directions
Teaching approach	Promote accuracy – correct errors
Interaction	Whole class work, suitable for large classes
Preparation	Write the names of family members on the board, e.g. *son, mother*. Write them randomly, i.e. not in the same order as the oral instructions. See Box 55.

Procedure

1 Say to the class *I am a famous queen, but I have a very strange family.*
2 Ask them to listen to your description of your family and to write the members of your family in a list, in the same order that they hear them, e.g. *Uncle, granddaughter*. Read from the script in Box 55.
3 When you have finished, check that the children have written the family names in the correct order.
4 Read the script again and ask the children to write the second part of the description, e.g. *Uncle – monster*.

Box 55   Family members

My **uncle** is a monster.
My **granddaughter** is a doll.
My **daughter** is a fairy.
My **cousin** is a robot.
My **son** is a pirate.
My **aunt** is a witch.
My **grandson** is a rabbit.
My **mother** is Cinderella.

Follow-up
The children create a family tree diagram showing the queen and her relatives. See Box 56. Ask the children to draw the relatives according to the descriptions in Box 55.

Box 56   Queen's family tree

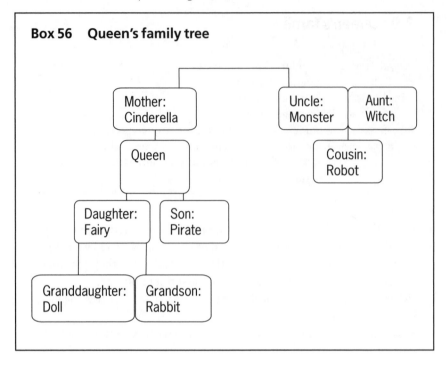

Follow-up
For other diagrams, see Activities 4.13, 5.17, 5.18, 6.15.

3.10 Fairy tale people

Level	**
Language focus	Comparatives and superlatives
Skills focus	Listening for details
Thinking focus	Sequencing
Teaching approach	Promote accuracy – correct errors
Interaction	Whole class work, suitable for large classes

Procedure
1 Tell the class that you are going to read out some information about the size of some magical fairy tale people.
2 You want the children to listen and write the names of these people in order of size, starting with the smallest and ending with the biggest.
3 It might help if they draw a long horizontal line across their page and place the magical people along this line as you read.

4 It is probably best if they use a pencil for this activity because they may want to change the order as you read.

5 Slowly and carefully read out the script from Box 57 and allow thinking time for the children to decide where they will write the name.

6 When you have finished, read all the sentences again for the children to check their answers.

7 The children then show their work to a partner and compare both the order and the spelling. See Box 58.

Box 57 Fairy tale people: script

The fairy is the smallest.
The monster is the biggest.
The giant is smaller than the monster and bigger than the pirate.
The frog is bigger than the fairy and smaller than the robot.
The robot is bigger than the frog and smaller than the witch.
The witch is smaller than the pirate.

Box 58 Fairy tale people: answers

Fairy	Frog	Robot	Witch	Pirate	Giant	Monster

3.11 Contrasting fairies and witches

Level	* *
Language focus	Antonyms, adjectives
Skills focus	Dictionary usage
Thinking focus	Differentiating
Teaching approach	Promote creativity – accept errors
Interaction	Pairwork, suitable for large classes
Preparation	On the board, draw a grid and write the headings from Box 59.

Procedure

1 Tell the children that although fairies and witches are both females with magical powers, they are very different.

2 Refer to the headings on the board and ask the children, in pairs, to help you complete the grid. Encourage them to use their dictionaries and class wallcharts to add a variety of descriptors.

Box 59   Fairies and witches

	Type of magic	Appearance	Clothes	Transport	Size	Tools for magic	Pets
Fairies	good, kind	beautiful, cute, pretty	bright, colourful, pink dress	wings	very small	wand	no pets
Witches	bad, evil	ugly, thin, large nose	black skirt and shirt or dress, hat	broomstick	same as a person	spells	black cat

---

Follow-up
- Ask the children to write sentences about how these two magical females differ. Tell them that *but* is a good contrast word to join their ideas, e.g. *Fairies are kind and good, but witches are bad and evil.*
- You could ask the children to tell you of stories they have read about bad fairies and good witches. They could make a new grid and include adjectives to describe these characters.

3.12 Three wishes

Level	* *
Language focus	Using hypothetical *would*
Skills focus	Speaking
Thinking focus	Making judgments
Teaching approach	Promote creativity – accept errors
Interaction	Individual work, pairwork and group work, suitable for large classes

Procedure
1 Tell the children that they have been granted three wishes.
2 Ask each child to write down three things that they would wish for, using the sentence stem *I would like . . .* or *I would like to . . .* Write these sentence stems on the board.

3 Now ask the children to work with a partner. This time, they can have only three wishes between them. Each pair should compare their wishes and choose the three most important wishes to keep.

4 Finally, join two pairs together to make a group of four. Each pair shares their three wishes and then the group must decide which three wishes their group wants to keep.

5 Ask the groups to tell the class about their three wishes.

Follow-up

There are a few interesting fairy tales about people who, when granted three wishes, waste the opportunity. One such story from Sweden is *The sausage*. See the Website appendix on page 148 for other fairy tales. Read some of these fairy tales to the children.

3.13 Jack and the beanstalk

Level	* * *
Language focus	Narrative, simple past tense
Skills focus	Reading
Thinking focus	Sequencing
Teaching approach	Promote accuracy – correct errors
Interaction	Whole class work, suitable for large classes
Preparation	On the board, copy the story summary formula from Box 60.

Procedure

1 Tell the children that the formula on the board represents a famous fairy tale.

2 Ask the children to suggest words that could be inserted into the formula. If they suggest a word that is part of the story summary, rub out the line and write in the word.

3 At the side of the board, keep a record of the children's suggestions, so that they do not repeat words.

4 If they have difficulties getting started, you may want to write in one or two words, e.g. *ogre*, *stalk* or *golden*.

5 Continue until the children have guessed all the missing words in the story summary.

Box 60   Jack and the beanstalk: story summary formula

Story summary formula	Story summary
_____ _____ _____ _____ _____ _____ _____ _____._____ _____ _____ _____ _____ _____ _____ _____ _____.	Jack stole a hen that laid golden eggs. Jack cut down the beanstalk and killed the ogre.

Follow-up

- Remove the story summary from the board and ask the children to write it in their own words.
- In this fairy story, Jack is seen as a hero who made his mother rich. However, from the ogre's point of view, Jack was a thief. Ask the children to rewrite the story from the ogre's point of view.
- For the on-line story of *Jack and the beanstalk*, check the Website appendix on page 148.
- For other narratives, see Activities 2.16, 3.5, 3.14, 3.18, 4.10, 5.1, 6.18.

3.14 Goldilocks

Level	* * *
Language focus	Narrative, simple past tense, *should*
Skills focus	Speaking and writing
Thinking focus	Analysing
Teaching approach	Promote creativity – accept errors
Interaction	Small group work, suitable for large classes
Preparation	Draw the problem-solving grid on the board and write in the headings. See Box 61.

Procedure

1   You could do this activity as pairwork, or you may prefer to put the children into small groups of three.

2 Briefly remind the class of the story of *Goldilocks and the three bears*.
   (See the Website appendix on page 149 for a link to the on-line story of
   Goldilocks.)

3 Then ask the children to think about the main character – Goldilocks.
   What were her problems? Ask the children to copy the problem-solving
   grid from the board and write in Goldilocks' problems, taking care to
   write the verb in the past tense.

4 Next, ask the children to think about how she tried to solve her
   problems. After discussion, they should record these solutions in the
   problem-solving grid, using past tense verbs.

5 Finally, ask the groups to discuss some advice they could give to
   Goldilocks. They then record these in the grid. Tell the children to use
   either *should* or *should not* in their advice.

Box 61   Goldilocks: problem-solving grid

Character	Problems	Solutions	Your suggestions
Goldilocks	She was hungry.	She ate Baby Bear's porridge.	You should not go into a stranger's house. You should not eat other people's food. You should not break other people's things. You should sleep in your own bed. You should write a note and apologise to the bears.
	She was tired.	She sat on Baby Bear's chair and broke it. She went to sleep in Baby Bear's bed.	
	She was frightened of the bears.	She ran away.	

Follow-up

- Ask the children to write a note from Goldilocks to the bears apologising
  for her poor behaviour.
- This activity could be done with any narrative which is familiar to the
  children. For other on-line stories, check the Website appendix on page
  149.
- For other narratives, see Activities 2.16, 3.5, 3.13, 3.18, 4.10, 5.1, 6.18.

3.15 Fortune telling

Level	* * *
Language focus	Conversation, future tense, adjectives
Skills focus	Speaking
Thinking focus	Imagining and inventing
Teaching approach	Promote creativity – accept errors
Interaction	Pairwork, suitable for large classes
Preparation	On the board, write the headings from Box 62, along with the sentence stems *You are going to . . .* and *I will . . .*

Procedure

1 Most children know about fortune telling either through palm reading, or the reading of cards or tea leaves, or simply gazing into a crystal ball. Tell the class that they are going to become fortune tellers.

2 Ask the children to add vocabulary to the grid on the board. Encourage the children to draw on their own vocabulary knowledge, using the headings as a guide.

3 Put the children into pairs. One person will be the fortune teller, and the other will respond to their predictions. Encourage the children to be imaginative as they invent scary scenarios and their corresponding plans for action.

4 The fortune teller chooses vocabulary from the grid to build a sentence following the pattern *You are going to . . .*

5 The partner replies by telling the fortune teller what he/she is going to do. Refer the children to the sentence stems on the board. See Box 63 for some possible answers.

6 Call on some of the pairs to share their conversation with the class.

Box 62   Vocabulary choices

Sense verbs	Adjectives to describe people	Fantasy characters	Setting: in the . . .
see, hear, **smell**, touch	clever, dangerous, **horrible**, kind, unfriendly, sad, beautiful, young, old, famous, hungry	ghost, princess, magician, frog, emperor, bat, **monster**, queen, king	cupboard, bedroom, garden, **fridge**, library, bathroom, mirror, kitchen, garden

---

Box 63   Sample answers

Fortune teller (prediction): You are going to **smell** a **horrible monster in the fridge**. What will you do?

Response (plan for action): I will quickly put on some gloves and carefully open the door of the fridge. If the monster is friendly, I will take him to the bathroom and tell him to take a shower.

3.16 House of horrors

Level	* * *
Language focus	Adjectives, simple present tense, prepositions of place
Skills focus	Listening for details
Thinking focus	Following directions
Teaching approach	Promote accuracy – correct errors
Interaction	Individual work, suitable for large classes

Procedure

1 Draw a blank grid on the board and ask the children to copy it onto their piece of paper. See Box 64.

2 Tell the children that this is a three-storey apartment building (or block of flats) consisting of a ground floor, a first floor and a second floor. It is called a 'house of horrors' because of the very strange people who live there. You may want to write some of the unfamiliar vocabulary like *wicked witch* on the board.

3 Tell the children that you are going to slowly and deliberately read out the descriptions of where the people live in the house of horrors. Ask them to listen carefully and write the name of the person on the correct apartment/flat. See Box 65.

4 Allow time for the children to process the information and to write the name of the occupant in the correct apartment/flat.

5 When you have finished, ask the children to compare their answers with the child sitting next to them.

Box 64   House of horrors grid

Second floor	Circus clown	Ugly monster	Untidy pirate
First floor	Wicked witch and black cat		Friendly witch
Ground floor	Dangerous dentist	Noisy singer	Horrible queen

© Cambridge University Press 2007

Box 65   House of horrors: descriptions

1 A noisy singer lives in the middle apartment/flat on the ground floor.
2 A wicked witch and her sister live on the first floor.
3 On the second floor, an ugly monster lives between an untidy pirate and a
   circus clown.
4 The apartment/flat above the noisy singer is empty.
5 A horrible queen lives on the right, next to the noisy singer.
6 The friendly witch lives between the untidy pirate and the horrible queen.
7 The wicked witch lives above the dangerous dentist.
8 The wicked witch lives with a black cat.

Follow-up
In pairs, children create their own house of horrors. One partner draws a
grid and the other tells his/her partner where all the strange occupants live.

3.17 The king's challenge

Level	* * *
Language focus	Discussion, question forms
Skills focus	Speaking
Thinking focus	Analysing a problem
Teaching approach	Promote creativity – accept errors
Interaction	Group work, suitable for large classes
Preparation	Either photocopy the king's challenge for each group, or write the challenge on the board or on a transparency. Give only the information in the shaded area. See Box 66.

Procedure

1 Divide the class into small groups.
2 Ask the children to read the challenge in the shaded area. See Box 66. Do
   not give them any extra information at this stage.
3 Tell the children that they have to decide whether to accept the king's
   challenge.
4 They can ask you questions if they need extra information. If they have
   trouble getting started, give them one of the sample questions from Box
   66. When they ask questions, give them details from the second part of
   Box 66 – Extra information. Of course, you can create as much extra
   information as you like.

5   After giving them some time to discuss the challenge, ask the groups to share their decision with the class. They should give reasons for deciding whether to accept or reject the king's challenge.

Box 66   Script: The king's challenge

The king has offered you and your friends a chance to go on an adventure. The king has told you that high in the mountains there is a cave which is full of gold. If you return in two days, the king will let you keep the gold. Should you take up the king's challenge?

Extra information: The season is autumn and the winter snow is not far away. The cave is one day's hike in the mountains, so you will have to take food and a tent and stay in the mountains overnight. There have been stories of wolves roaming in the mountains. Gold is very heavy. The local people are kind and helpful.

Sample questions: How far is it? What's the weather like? How long will it take? How heavy is the gold? What will we have to take? Are there any dangers? Can anyone help us?

© Cambridge University Press 2007

Follow-up

- To extend some of your more able students, draw the SWOT analysis grid on the board. See Box 67. Explain that this grid will help them to analyse the problem in greater depth. Use some of the stimulus questions to illustrate the sort of information that belongs in each section of the grid. The children write notes from their discussion in the SWOT analysis grid. When they have finished their analysis, ask the groups to decide if they will take up the king's challenge. They should explain their decision to the class.
- This way of analysing a problem can be used to discuss any problems in the class – either real problems, or problems which arise in story plots.

Box 67   SWOT analysis stimulus questions

STRENGTHS: What are the strengths of your group? Are you brave and clever? Can you climb in the mountains? Are you strong and fit?	**WEAKNESSES:** What are your weaknesses? Are you afraid of heights? Do you think you are too young for this challenge? Will you be strong enough to carry your rucksack?
OPPORTUNITIES: What could you learn from this challenge?	**THREATS:** What are some of the problems you could face?

3.18 Create a fantasy tale

Level	* * *
Language focus	Narrative, simple past tense
Skills focus	Speaking
Thinking focus	Combining ideas
Teaching approach	Promote creativity – accept errors
Interaction	Team work, suitable for large classes
Preparation	Draw the story grid on the board. See Box 68.

Procedure

1 Divide the class into two teams. In large classes, you could do this activity with nine teams.

2 Tell the children that they have to invent a story outline, using the elements in the grid. You may have to explain unfamiliar vocabulary from the grid. The rules of the game are that they can choose words that go across the grid, down the grid, or diagonally. (This game is like Noughts and crosses, or Tick–tack–toe.)

3 If a team can invent a story while keeping within the rules of the game, they win a point and the other team has a turn.

4 The game should continue until all possible stories have been suggested. The team with the most story outlines is the winner.

Box 68   Story grid

witch	black cat	book of spells
poison	haunted house	ghost
kidnapped children	stormy night	lost traveller

Follow-up

- Ask the children to choose their favourite story outline and write the story. They then illustrate the story and display it in the classroom.
- For other narratives, see Activities 2.16, 3.5, 3.13, 3.14, 4.10, 5.1, 6.18.

4 The world around us

4.1 Rivers of the world

Level	*
Language focus	Vocabulary: names of rivers, letters of the alphabet
Skills focus	Listening for details
Thinking focus	Recognising and writing letters
Teaching approach	Promote accuracy – correct errors
Interaction	Whole class work, suitable for large classes

Procedure

1 Explain to the class that you are going to read out the names of some famous rivers in the world.

2 Tell the children that you will spell out the name of each river, and as you say the letters, you want them to write the name of the river. You will say each letter once, so they have to listen carefully the first time. Make sure they know to begin each word with a capital letter.

3 Choose one river from Box 69 and say the name of the river first. Then carefully spell out the word, allowing time for the children to write it. When spelling out *Mississippi*, you should say *double s* and *double p*.

4 When you have spelled out all the names of rivers from Box 69, choose children to write the correct spelling on the board for the others to check their answers.

Box 69   World rivers

A–M–A–Z–O–N	South America
N–I–L–E	Africa
D–A–N–U–B–E	Germany/Europe
G–A–N–G–E–S	India/Asia
M–I–S–S–I–S–S–I–P–P–I	The United States
S–E–I–N–E	France/Europe
Y–A–N–G–T–S–E	China/Asia

Follow-up
- Ask the children to sort the rivers into alphabetical order.
- Ask the children to use an atlas to find these rivers. Then ask them to note the country or continent through which the rivers flow. They could also discover which river is the longest and which is the shortest.

4.2 Map making

Level	*
Language focus	Map, geography words, letters of the alphabet, numbers
Skills focus	Listening for details
Thinking focus	Labelling
Teaching approach	Promote accuracy – correct errors
Interaction	Pairwork, suitable for large classes
Preparation	Draw a map-making grid on the board. See Box 70.

Procedure

1   Divide the class into pairs and ask each pair to copy the map-making grid from the board. See Box 70. You may want to introduce new vocabulary from Box 71 before you begin the activity.
2   Tell the class that they are going to draw a map and they have to listen for two pieces of information.
3   One person in the pair has to listen for the coordinate, which will be a combination of one letter and one number, e.g. C3. The other person has to listen for the geographical feature, e.g. *A big blue lake.*
4   Together, they combine their information and draw the geographical feature on their map-making grid.

Box 70   Map-making grid

4					
3					
2					
1					
	A	B	C	D	E

Box 71   Map-making instructions

At C3 draw a big blue lake.
At A1 draw a small green mountain.
At E1 draw a big brown mountain.
At B3 draw a long beach.
At B4 draw a blue sea.
A river flows from E1 to C3.

Follow-up
- Ask the pairs to prepare their own map. They take turns to give map-making instructions to their partner, who draws their map on a map-making grid. When they have finished, they compare maps and check that their partner has followed their directions.
- If you want to practise other numbers or letters, change the coordinates. For example, you may want to have numbers from 6 to 10, and letters from L to P.

4.3 Drawing my natural world

Level	*
Language focus	Prepositions of place, present continuous tense
Skills focus	Reading and speaking
Thinking focus	Illustrating and interpreting
Teaching approach	Promote accuracy – correct errors
Interaction	Whole class work, suitable for large classes
Preparation	Write the sentences from Box 72 onto separate pieces of paper.

Procedure

1 Divide the class into groups with three children in each group.
2 Ask one child from each group to come to the front of the class, and show them a sentence from Box 72. Each child should see the same sentence clue.
3 They return to their groups and, without speaking, draw the information you have shown them.
4 The first group to guess the answer and correctly say the sentence wins a point.

5 Then the next person in each group has a chance to read one of your sentences and draw the information for their group.

6 Continue until all group members have had a chance to participate.

Box 72   Having fun in nature: sentences

1 He/She is flying **over** a *mountain*.
2 He/She is jumping **in** a *river*.
3 He/She is riding **around** an *island* on a bike.
4 He/She is running **on** a *beach*.
5 He/She is swimming **under** the *sea*.
6 He/She is swimming **across** a *lake*.
7 He/She is walking **behind** a *waterfall*.
8 He/She is sitting **on** a *mountain*.

4.4 North, south, east and west

Level	*
Language focus	Chant, vocabulary: names of cities and countries
Skills focus	Speaking: stress patterns
Thinking focus	Inventing
Teaching approach	Promote accuracy – correct errors
Interaction	Whole class work, suitable for large classes

Procedure

1 Point to the north and ask the children to copy you and say *North*.

2 Now point to the south, the east and then the west, and each time ask the children to point and say the word.

3 Together, chant **North, *south*, *east and west*** in a singsong style, taking care to stress all words except *and*. Each time the children say a direction, get them to point in that direction.

4 Next, ask the children to name a favourite place in the world. It could be their own town or country, or it could be a place they would like to visit.

5 Write the place on the board and make a note of the number of syllables it has and where the stress falls. See Box 73 for some examples.

6 Add this place to the chant. The children will now say something like **North, *south*, *east and west*, *Spain is the place that I like best*.** Ask the children to point in the direction of north, south, east and west for the

first part of the chant, and clap on the stressed syllables in the second part of the chant. The stressed syllables are in bold.

7 Continue to add new places to the chant.

Box 73 Chanting about places

Chant	Places with stress on the first syllable	Places with stress on the second syllable	Places with single syllable
North, south, east and **west,** ... is the **place** that **I** like **best.**	**Chi**na **Par**is **Swe**den **Lon**don	Bra**zil** Ber**lin** Du**bai** New **York**	France Rome Greece Spain

---

Follow-up

- Vary the chant from the first person to the third person, making sure the children pronounce the third person *s* sound and continue to note the stressed syllables.
- The children use their atlases to find the places in their chant.
- For other chants and raps, see Activities 1.11, 2.7, 4.6, 5.1, 5.7, 6.1.

4.5 Geographical tongue twisters

Level	*
Language focus	Word order in a simple sentence
Skills focus	Pronunciation: initial consonants
Thinking focus	Constructing
Teaching approach	Promote accuracy – correct errors
Interaction	Team work, suitable for large classes

Procedure

1 Divide the class into two teams.

2 On the board, write the verb *is bouncing* and the geographical place *beach*.

3 Team 1 suggests a subject for the verb *is bouncing*, e.g. *A ball*. The aim of the competition is to suggest words starting with *b*.

4 Team 2 suggests another word to add to the sentence. The sentence could now read *A big ball is bouncing . . . beach*.

5   The first team may want to change the sentence to make *A big ball* the object. In this way, they could add another *b* word as a subject, e.g. *Ben is bouncing a big ball . . . beach.*

6   Each team continues to add a *b* word to the sentence. The last team to add a word is the winner. See Box 74 for some sentence ideas.

7   It is important to pay attention to the grammatical accuracy of the children's suggestions and make corrections where necessary.

8   Finally, the class reads the tongue twister aloud.

Box 74   Sample tongue twisters

B	Ben's brother **is bouncing** a big ball on a blue and black boat beside a beautiful **beach**.
W	A woman **is walking** and watching a wonderful **waterfall**.
F	Five fathers and their friends **are fishing** for their favourite fish in the **forest**.
S	Sad Sam's sister Sue and six small snakes **are swimming** in the **sea**.

Follow-up

• Choose other letters of the alphabet and ask pairs to create new tongue twisters. Each time, write the verb and the geographical place. Each team has a turn to add a new word to make a sentence. See Box 74.

• Display the tongue twisters in the classroom and regularly ask the children to say them aloud. Alternatively, you could create a class book of tongue twisters.

4.6 Sphere shapes

Level	*
Language focus	Chant, vocabulary: spherical objects
Skills focus	Speaking
Thinking focus	Recalling and sequencing
Teaching approach	Promote creativity – accept errors
Interaction	Small group work, suitable for large classes
Preparation	For this activity, you will need to bring a spherical object, e.g. a ball, to class.

Procedure

1 Hold up the ball and tell the class that it is the shape of a sphere. Write the word *Sphere* on the board. Say the word *Sphere* and ask the class to say the word after you.
2 Tell them that our world is also a sphere.
3 In small groups, get the children to write any other objects they know of that are in the shape of a sphere.
4 Ask the groups to share their answers and write the words on the board. See Box 75 for some suggestions.
5 Then ask the groups to sequence the spheres from the largest to the smallest.

Box 75   Sphere words

apple, onion, orange, pea, potato, tomato, tennis ball, basket ball, table-tennis ball, eye, head, sun, moon

---

Follow-up

* Teach the children the chant about spheres. See Box 76. The stressed syllables are in bold. Ask the children to stamp their feet on the stressed syllables, and spin around on the words *spin, spin, spin*. For the last line, they clap and stamp on the stressed syllables.
* You could adapt this activity by asking the children to find examples of other shapes, like cubes, cylinders, squares or circles.
* For other chants and raps, see Activities 1.11, 2.7, 4.4, 5.1, 5.7, 6.1.

Box 76   Sphere chant

Apples and **on**ions,
The **moon** and the **sun**.
These are **spheres** – every **one**.
The **world** is a **sphere** – **spin, spin, spin**.
The **world** is the **sphere** that **we** live **in**!

4.7 New Year celebrations

Level	**
Language focus	Vocabulary: size, colour, adjectives, nouns, names of countries
Skills focus	Listening for details
Thinking focus	Sorting
Teaching approach	Promote accuracy – correct errors
Interaction	Group work
Preparation	Photocopy the listening grids for the children to complete. Their copies should contain only the headings in the shaded areas of the grid. See Box 77.

Procedure

1 Tell the class that people all over the world celebrate the New Year in different ways. If you have time, ask them to tell you briefly how they celebrate the New Year.

2 Divide the class into teams with four children in each team. Allocate one of the headings to each member of the team: size, colour, other adjective and noun. See Box 77.

3 Tell the children that each person in the team has to listen for different key words.

4 Read out the sentences from Box 78, allowing enough time for each member to write down their key word and complete the listening grid.

Note: In this activity, check that the less able learners listen for vocabulary like size or colour, and the more advanced learners listen for the other adjective or the noun.

Box 77   Listening grid

Size	Colour	Other adjective	Noun	Place
small	red	square	envelopes	**China**
big	white	round	rice cakes	**Korea**
small	brown	sweet	doughnuts	**Holland**
very small	yellow and black	soft	peas	**United States**
small	green	tasty	12 grapes	**Spain**
long	yellow	thin	noodles	**Japan**

© Cambridge University Press 2007

Box 78   International New Year celebrations

1 In Spain we eat 12 small, tasty, green grapes on New Year's Eve.
2 People in the south of the United States eat very small, yellow and black, soft peas to bring them good luck in the New Year.
3 Every Chinese New Year, our parents give us a small, red, square envelope with money inside it.
4 On New Year's Eve in Japan, people eat long, thin, yellow noodles.
5 Korean people eat big, white, round rice cakes on New Year's Day.
6 In Holland we enjoy eating small, brown, sweet doughnuts to celebrate the New Year.

4.8 New Year's Day emails

Level	**
Language focus	Email, simple present tense
Skills focus	Reading and writing
Thinking focus	Producing and inventing
Teaching approach	Promote creativity – accept errors
Interaction	Individual work, suitable for large classes
Preparation	Photocopy or make an overhead transparency of the text. See Box 79.

Procedure

1 Tell the class that a pen pal from Australia has written to them, asking them about how they celebrate the New Year. Show them the text from Box 79.
2 Ask them to write a brief reply. Useful sentence stems from the email are in bold. Encourage the children to use these sentence stems in their reply email.

Note: If you prefer, you could jointly construct a class email reply. In this case, you ask the children to make suggestions and you write these on the board. Then, together, you make corrections and think about ways to improve the email.

Box 79   Email from Australia

Hi

We are the children in Year 5 **at** Sunshine Beach Primary School. **Every New Year**, hundreds of people come to our beach to celebrate the New Year. **We usually** have a party **on New Year's Eve and all the kids** can stay awake until midnight. **The next day**, everyone is very tired.

How do you celebrate the New Year?

© Cambridge University Press 2007

Follow-up

For other cards, letters and emails, see Activities 2.12, 5.11, 5.15, 6.8.

4.9   Loy Krathong Festival from Thailand

Level	**
Language focus	Description, simple present tense
Skills focus	Note taking
Thinking focus	Differentiating
Teaching approach	Promote accuracy – correct errors
Interaction	Pairwork, suitable for large classes
Preparation	Photocopy the brief description of the Loy Krathong Festival. See Box 80. Draw the note-taking grid on the board and write in the questions. See Box 81.

Procedure

1   Give each pair the short description of the Loy Krathong Festival from Thailand. See Box 80. If you have a world map, show the children where Thailand is.

2   Ask the children to complete the note-taking grid. This will encourage them to read for specific details, as opposed to copying whole sentences. It is also important to emphasise that you do not expect them to recognise every word, but to make inferences about the meanings of words from the context of the paragraph.

3   When the children have finished, complete the note-taking grid on the board.

Box 80   Loy Krathong Festival

The Loy Krathong Festival is a famous festival in Thailand. It happens during the full moon in the twelfth month. The Thai people make a Krathong boat from banana leaves. They put candles, flowers and money into the boat. In the moonlight, they put their Krathongs into the river and hope that all their bad luck will float away.

© Cambridge University Press 2007

Box 81   Loy Krathong: note-taking grid

Question	Notes
1 Where is the festival? (Two words)	1 Thailand, river
2 When is the festival? (Two words + two words)	2 Full moon, twelfth month
3 Why do they have the festival? (Five words)	3 Bad luck will float away
4 What is a Krathong? (One word)	4 Boat
5 What is a Krathong made of? (Two words)	5 Banana leaves
6 What is in the Krathong? (Three words)	6 Candles, flowers, money

Follow-up
- Ask each pair, from their notes, to write their own description of the Loy Krathong Festival.
- Children who are particularly interested in international festivals may like to conduct further research into this famous Thai festival.
- Get the children to make their own Krathongs and have a Loy Krathong Festival beside a river or pool of water.

4.10 Pinocchio: an Italian story

Level	**
Language focus	Narrative, comparatives and superlatives
Skills focus	Pronunciation: word stress
Thinking focus	Recalling
Teaching approach	Promote accuracy – correct errors
Interaction	Whole class work, suitable for large classes
Preparation	On the board, write the children's part of the story telling. See Box 82.

Procedure

1 Divide the class into three groups. Explain that you are going to tell them a very old story from Italy, and that you want them to join in. You may want to explain vocabulary such as *puppet* and *lie* before you start to tell the story.

2 With dramatic expression, begin to tell the story of Pinocchio.

3 When you get to the part when the children join in, point to Group 1 and then to their lines on the board. Encourage the children to use gestures to show how the nose becomes longer each time.

4 Point to Group 2 to join in the chant, and then to Group 3. Each time the volume of the story increases as another group joins in the chant.

5 Finally, the whole class joins in the last part of the story.

Box 82   Pinocchio story telling

Participants	Story
Teacher	Once upon a time, an old man called Geppetto made a puppet from a piece of wood. Then one day, the puppet started to walk and talk. His name was Pinocchio. One day, Pinocchio told his father a lie. His nose started to grow.
Children: Group 1	He told another lie and his nose grew longer.
Children: Groups 1 and 2	He told another lie and his nose grew longer and longer.
Children: Groups 1, 2 and 3	He told another lie and his nose grew longer and longer and longer.
Children: Together	Soon he had the longest nose in the village.

Follow-up

- Check your library for the complete story of Pinocchio. Try to find an illustrated version of the story and read it to the class.
- For other narratives, see Activities 2.16, 3.5, 3.13, 3.14, 3.18, 5.1, 6.18.

4.11 Carnival in Brazil

Level	**
Language focus	Description, simple present tense
Skills focus	Listening for key words
Thinking focus	Identifying and selecting
Teaching approach	Promote creativity – accept errors
Interaction	Group work, suitable for large classes

Procedure

1 Remind the class of the steps in a dictogloss. See Activity 2.15 for detailed instructions.
2 Ask them to recall carnivals or festivals in their own country.
3 Read out the description of a carnival in Brazil at a slow and steady pace. See Box 83. Remember, the pace must be a little faster than a dictation.
4 While you are reading, the children are writing key words from the text.

5 When you have finished reading, ask small groups of children to reconstruct the original text.

6 At the end of the activity, the children compare their descriptions with the original text.

Box 83   Description of a Brazilian carnival

Every year, people in Brazil have a big party. It goes on for four days and four nights. They have a lot of loud music and dancing and wear colourful shirts and dresses and scarves. Everyone is happy because they are on holiday.

Follow-up

Ask the groups to glue their sentences on a piece of cardboard and display their work in the classroom. Include a copy of the original description from Box 83. The children might also enjoy creating a carnival atmosphere by decorating their work with illustrations, balloons and streamers.

4.12 Popular Asian game

Level	* *
Language focus	Procedure, imperatives, comparatives
Skills focus	Reading instructions
Thinking focus	Recalling
Teaching approach	Promote creativity – accept errors
Interaction	Group work, suitable for large classes
Preparation	Either photocopy or write the instructions on an overhead transparency. See Box 84.

The game of Paper, scissors, stone is a popular game in Asia. It is used by children to make decisions such as who will go first. The instructions in Box 84 are a variation of this game.

Procedure

1 Put the children into groups of three.

2 Ask them to read the instructions from Box 84.

3 Then ask the children to play the game. You will know if they have comprehended the instructions by how successfully they play the game.

Box 84   Ant, person, elephant

Instructions

Put out your little finger. Little finger = ant
Put out your pointing finger. Pointing finger = person
Put out your thumb. Thumb = elephant

Play the game

Count *One, two, three* and everyone must quickly put out **one** finger.

Who is the winner?

An **ant** can climb into an **elephant**'s ear and bite it, so an **ant** is stronger than an **elephant**.
An **elephant** can stand on a **person** and hurt him/her, so an **elephant** is stronger than a **person**.
A **person** can stand on an **ant** and squash it, so a **person** is stronger than an **ant**.

© Cambridge University Press 2007

Follow-up
For other procedures, see Activities 2.9, 3.4, 4.15, 4.18, 5.8, 6.10, 6.13, 6.16.

4.13 Natural disasters

Level	* * *
Language focus	Vocabulary: geography and weather
Skills focus	Listening and speaking
Thinking focus	Sorting, matching and justifying
Teaching approach	Promote creativity – accept errors
Interaction	Group work, suitable for large classes
Preparation	Draw the diagram on the board. See Box 86.

Procedure

1 Briefly explain the meaning of each of the natural disasters given in the diagram on the board. You may want to use the children's first language to do this. See Box 86.
2 Divide the class into small groups and ask each group to draw the diagram from the board.
3 Next, ask the children to listen to the vocabulary as you read out each word. See Box 85. Tell them you want them to sort the vocabulary according to the natural disasters in the diagram. See Box 86.

4 Allow the children time to discuss where they want to allocate each vocabulary item. They write the vocabulary item next to the natural disaster in the diagram.

5 When they have finished, ask each group to share their answers with the class. There will obviously be some words that fit into a number of categories, e.g. *hot* could apply equally to *forest fire*, *volcano* or *drought*. Provided that the group can justify their choices, accept the answers. Sample answers are in Box 87.

Box 85 Natural disasters vocabulary

wind, white, burn, rain, crack, cold, dry, water, mountain, river, black, cloud, snow, red, boat, ice, hot, shake

---

Box 86 Natural disasters

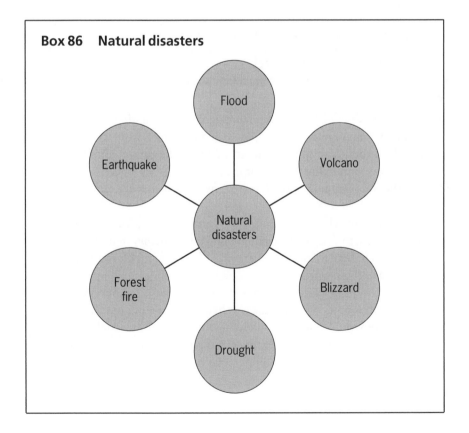

Box 87   Natural disaster answers

Flood	Volcano	Blizzard	Drought	Forest fire	Earthquake
rain, water, river, cloud, boat	burn, mountain, black, cloud, red, hot	wind, white, cold, cloud, snow, ice	dry, hot	wind, burn, black, red, hot	crack, shake

---

4.14 Pompeii

Level	* * *
Language focus	Information report, simple past tense
Skills focus	Reading: words in context
Thinking focus	Analysing
Teaching approach	Promote accuracy – correct errors
Interaction	Small group work, suitable for large classes
Preparation	Photocopy the information report about Pompeii for each group. See Box 88.

Procedure

1   Ask the children to quickly skim through the information report about Pompeii. Point out that at first they won't recognise every word, but you will show them how to use context clues to make guesses about the meaning of unfamiliar vocabulary.

2   Ask the children, as they read, to note five words that are unfamiliar to them.

3   Then divide the class into small groups and encourage the children, in their groups, to discuss the meaning of the vocabulary items they have chosen. Tell them to look at other parts of the text for clues about the meaning of these words.

4   Ask the groups to share their answers with the class. Encourage them to explain what other words in the text helped them work out the meanings.

5   Finally, for words that still remain a problem, use the textual clues to show the children how to infer the meanings from the context. See Box 89.

Box 88   Pompeii: information report

Pompeii was a city in Italy. In 79 AD, during the first century, a dangerous volcano called Vesuvius began to throw out molten rock. This is called lava. The red hot lava, which looked like a river, flowed down the mountain and over the city. Sixteen centuries later, people discovered Pompeii and started to dig up the old city.

© Cambridge University Press 2007

Box 89   Pompeii: words and context clues

Words	Context clues
Pompeii	City in Italy
century/centuries	79 AD, first, sixteen centuries later
	(Background knowledge: cents, centimetre = 100 . . .)
volcano	Throw out, dangerous, molten rock, lava, red, hot, flowed, mountain
Vesuvius	Has a capital letter, so must be a proper noun, volcano called . . .
molten	Red, hot, looked like a river
lava	Red, hot, This is called . . .
flowed	River, it's a verb describing what a river does

Follow-up

- You may have some children who would like to explore the story of Pompeii further. Encourage them to do Internet searches or to borrow from their school library. Ask them to give a short talk to the class about their research findings.
- For other information reports, see Activities 1.7, 1.8, 1.13, 2.8, 2.18.

4.15 Safety guidelines

Level	***
Language focus	Procedure, suggestions and obligations, modal verbs
Skills focus	Speaking
Thinking focus	Proposing
Teaching approach	Promote creativity – accept errors
Interaction	Small group work, suitable for large classes

Note: This subject may need to be treated with sensitivity.

Procedure

1   On the board, write the natural disasters from Box 86. If the children do not know these words in English, provide the meaning in their first language.

2   Say to the children *If we had a . . . at our school, what would we do?* Choose a natural disaster from the list on the board.

3   Divide the class into two teams, with one team focussing on the things they **should do**, and the other team focussing on the things they **must not do**.

4   Within each team, create small 'buzz' groups of two or three children. Give them two minutes to come up with some suggestions and then ask them to share these with their team.

5   Then record their suggestions on the board.

Note: You could either use this as a genuine opportunity to revise a safety drill, e.g. a fire drill, or you could ask the children to use their background knowledge from the TV news to propose possible safety rules.

Follow-up

- Create a class safety chart and display the children's rules in the classroom.
- Ask the children to email a school in a place where these natural disasters occur. What safety measures do these schools have in place?
- For other procedures, see Activities 2.9, 3.4, 4.12, 4.18, 5.8, 6.10, 6.13, 6.16.

4.16 Current affairs recount

Level	* * *
Language focus	Recount, simple past tense, vocabulary: geography
Skills focus	Writing
Thinking focus	Creating
Teaching approach	Promote creativity – accept errors
Interaction	Pairwork, suitable for large classes
Preparation	Write the sentence stems and writing prompts on the board. See Box 90.

Procedure

1   On the board, write the natural disasters from Box 86. If the children do not know these words in English, provide the meaning in their first language.

2 Ask the children to recall any images of natural disasters from recent television news broadcasts.

3 Using the sentence stems and writing prompts from Box 90, ask the children, in pairs, to construct a small current affairs recount. Encourage them to talk together and decide on the most suitable language for their recount.

Box 90   Natural disasters: sentence stems

I saw a ... (Natural disaster) on TV ... (When?)
It was in ... (Where?)
The people had to ... (What did they do?)
There was / There were ... (Write one sentence about the buildings, animals or plants.)

Follow-up

- Ask the pairs of children to swap their recounts with another pair. Each pair then reads through the work of their peers and makes suggestions about vocabulary, grammar, punctuation, or other ideas to add. The children return their work to the original owners, who edit their draft and prepare their recounts for display in the classroom.
- This activity would work better if you were able to give the children a few days' warning, so that they could pay special attention to news items on television.
- For other factual recounts, see Activities 1.17, 5.14.

4.17 Earthquakes and floods

Level	* * *
Language focus	Personal recount, simple past and past continuous tenses, time-sequencing signals
Skills focus	Reading for main idea
Thinking focus	Analysing, sequencing
Teaching approach	Promote accuracy – correct errors
Interaction	Group work, suitable for large classes
Preparation	Either photocopy the sentences from Box 91, or write them on an overhead transparency. If you have time, you could cut the text into the sentence strips.

Note: This subject may need to be treated with sensitivity.

Procedure

1 Write the words *Earthquake* and *Flood* on the board and check that the children know the meaning of these words.

2 Divide the class into small groups and tell the children that you want them to read some information about earthquakes and floods. The information is in the form of a personal recount. The problem is that the sentences have been mixed up. It is their task to sort the sentences into two groups: earthquakes and floods.

3 Encourage the children to talk about their choices when deciding where each sentence belongs. They do not have to rewrite the sentences – just sort them into two groups.

4 Call on groups to read out their answers.

Box 91   Personal recounts: combined sentences

Combined sentences	Personal recount answers
1 Quickly we ran downstairs and into the street.	**Earthquake** We were inside when suddenly we saw all the books falling onto the floor. Quickly we ran downstairs and into the street.
2 Then, last night, the water in the river flowed into the town.	
3 There we saw cracks in the ground everywhere.	
4 It was raining for days and days and the river was getting higher and higher.	There we saw cracks in the ground everywhere. **Flood** It was raining for days and days and the river was getting higher and higher.
5 We were inside when suddenly we saw all the books falling onto the floor.	
6 A boat came and took us to safety.	Then, last night, the water in the river flowed into the town. A boat came and took us to safety.

© Cambridge University Press 2007

Follow-up

• When the children have sorted the sentences into two groups (earthquakes and floods), ask them to organise the sentences into the correct order to form two personal recounts.

• For other personal recounts, see Activities 1.10, 2.13, 2.15.

4.18 Emergency procedures

Level	* * *
Language focus	Procedure, imperatives
Skills focus	Listening for nouns and verbs
Thinking focus	Sorting information
Teaching approach	Promote accuracy – correct errors
Interaction	Pairwork, suitable for large classes
Preparation	Make an overhead transparency of the cloze activity in Box 92.

Note: This subject may need to be treated with sensitivity.

Procedure

1 Tell the class that you are going to read out some emergency procedures. This is what people have to do when a hurricane or a cyclone is approaching. Choose the appropriate word for your area, i.e. *hurricane* or *cyclone*, and check that they know the meaning of these words.

2 Ask the children to form into pairs. One person has to listen for all the nouns, and the other person has to listen for all the verbs. In this activity, listening for the verbs is easier than listening for the nouns, so allocate the verbs to your less able learners.

3 Now slowly and carefully read out the emergency procedures from Box 92.

4 Finally, call on the children to give their answers and complete the cloze on the overhead transparency.

Box 92 Hurricane/Cyclone safety instructions

Emergency procedures	Safety procedure: cloze activity	Verbs	Nouns
Preparation: Buy some batteries for your radio and your torch, as well as some canned food.	**Preparation:** 1 . . . some batteries for your 2 . . . and your 3 . . ., as well as some canned 4 . . .	1 Buy	2 radio 3 torch 4 food
Fill some large bottles with drinking water.	5 . . . some large 6 . . . with drinking 7 . . .	5 Fill	6 bottles 7 water
During the cyclone/hurricane: Listen to the radio or TV for information. Go to the strongest part of your home, for example, the bathroom, cellar or hall.	**During the cyclone/hurricane:** 8 . . . to the 9 . . . or TV for information. 10 . . . to the strongest part of your home, for example, the 11 . . ., cellar or 12 . . .	8 Listen 10 Go	9 radio 11 bathroom 12 hall

© Cambridge University Press 2007

Follow-up

- If you have extra time, you could use the lists of nouns and verbs to jointly construct a list of emergency procedures, similar to those in Box 92. To construct a text jointly, call upon children in the class to suggest the sentences that you should write on the board. Do not correct their work, but write it as they say it. When the text is finished, look at it together and ask the children to suggest ways of improving it. This could include making corrections to grammar, changing vocabulary choices, or altering the order of the sentences.
- For other procedures, see Activities 2.9, 3.4, 4.12, 4.15, 5.8, 6.10, 6.13, 6.16.

5 Healthy bodies

5.1 Grandma! What big eyes you've got!

Level	*
Language focus	Narrative, vocabulary: parts of the body
Skills focus	Speaking: fluency and expression
Thinking focus	Combining ideas
Teaching approach	Promote creativity – accept errors
Interaction	Team work, suitable for large classes
Preparation	On the board, write only the first sentence of the chant, for both Little Red Riding Hood and the Big Bad Wolf. See Box 93.

Procedure

1 Tell the children that together they are going to act out part of the story of *Little Red Riding Hood*. If they do not know the story, tell them briefly that a Big Bad Wolf is dressed up in Grandma's clothes and is sitting up in Grandma's bed when Little Red Riding Hood comes to bring gifts to her grandmother. She is surprised to see the change in her grandmother's appearance and has a conversation with the wolf.

2 Divide the class into two teams. One half of the class will play the part of Little Red Riding Hood and the other half will play the part of the Big Bad Wolf.

3 The first team begins by reading from the board *Oh, Grandma! What big eyes you've got!* Encourage the children to speak with great surprise. See Box 93.

4 The second team then has to read out what the wolf does with his eyes, e.g. *See*. They then chant back *All the better to see you, my dear*. The wolf's tone suggests that he is only pretending to be friendly and charming.

5 The first team then chooses another part of the body. Note that only the first sentence of the chant is on the board. From here on, the children use the pattern of the first sentence and add their own suggestions. They continue their chant: *Oh, Grandma! What big . . . you've got!* Make sure they leave *teeth* until the very last.

6 The second team decides what the wolf could do with this part of the body, and they chant back *All the better to . . ., my dear!*

7   The chant continues until they come to the teeth. This is the climax of
    the story, when the wolf reveals his true intentions, i.e. to eat Little
    Red Riding Hood. Encourage the children to really dramatise this part of
    the story.

Box 93   Little Red Riding Hood chant

Little Red Riding Hood	The Big Bad Wolf
Oh, Grandma! What big **eyes** you've got!	All the better to **see/look at** you, my dear.
Oh, Grandma! What big **ears** you've got!	All the better to **hear** you, my dear.
Oh, Grandma! What a big **nose** you've got!	All the better to **smell** you, my dear.
Oh, Grandma! What big **feet** you've got!	All the better to **run** with you, my dear.
Oh, Grandma! What big **arms** you've got!	All the better to **catch/hug** you, my dear.
Oh, Grandma! What big **hands** you've got!	All the better to **draw** with you, my dear.
Oh, Grandma! What big **legs** you've got!	All the better to **jump** with you, my dear.
Oh, Grandma! What a big **mouth** you've got!	All the better to **sing/talk** with you, my dear.
Oh, Grandma! What big **teeth** you've got!	All the better to **eat** you, my dear!

Follow-up
- Find a picture story book of *Little Red Riding Hood* and read it to the
  class.
- For other narratives, see Activities 2.16, 3.5, 3.13, 3.14, 3.18, 4.10, 6.18.

5.2 Callisthenics

Level	*
Language focus	Instructions, vocabulary: parts of the body, shapes
Skills focus	Speaking and listening
Thinking focus	Following directions
Teaching approach	Promote accuracy – correct errors
Interaction	Whole class work, suitable for large classes
Preparation	On the board, draw a circle, a square and a triangle. Write the English words beside each shape.

Procedure

1 Ask the children to stand up and give them one of the instructions from Box 94, e.g. *Draw a big circle with your head*. The idea is that they can stretch and exercise while they listen to directions and revise the names of the parts of the body.

2 When they have grasped the idea of the activity, call on one of the children to give instructions to the others, e.g. *Draw a small square with your right foot*.

3 Each child who has a turn to give instructions then chooses someone else to give the next instruction.

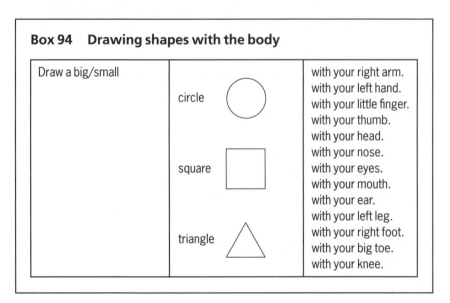

Box 94   Drawing shapes with the body

Draw a big/small		with your right arm.
	circle ◯	with your left hand.
		with your little finger.
		with your thumb.
		with your head.
		with your nose.
	square ▢	with your eyes.
		with your mouth.
		with your ear.
		with your left leg.
	triangle △	with your right foot.
		with your big toe.
		with your knee.

5.3 Create your own dance

Level	*
Language focus	Instructions, vocabulary: parts of the body, action verbs
Skills focus	Speaking, listening and reading
Thinking focus	Inventing
Teaching approach	Promote creativity – accept errors
Interaction	Pairwork, suitable for large classes
Preparation	Choose a music CD – something you know the children will love to dance to.

Procedure

1 Tell the children that, together, you are going to create a new dance routine. Play some of the music and suggest the first set of actions, e.g. *Put your hands on your arms and tap, tap, tap with your fingers.* Write this sentence on the board, and get the children to do the actions.

2 Give the children a few seconds to talk with their partner about what actions could come next. Some suggestions are in Box 95. Then choose one of the children to suggest a dance move.

3 As each new set of movements is suggested, write them on the board. The children may not have the language to fully express what they want to do. Encourage them to say as much as they can in English, and then supply the missing words for them.

4 As you write the dance instructions on the board, ask the children to read them and do the actions.

5 Finally, play the music and have the whole class moving, tapping, jumping and generally having a wonderful time.

Box 95   Dance movements

Parts of the body	Movements	
Put your hands on your arms	Wiggle	Run
Put your hands on your head	Tap	Walk
Put your hands on your ears	Shake	Spin
Put your hands on your knees	Kick	Point
Put your hands on your feet	Clap	Bounce
Put your knee on your nose	Jump	Fly like a bird
Put your foot on your leg		

5.4 Healthy morning routine

Level	*
Language focus	Song, vocabulary: parts of the body, personal hygiene
Skills focus	Speaking: rhythm, stress
Thinking focus	Inventing
Teaching approach	Promote creativity – accept errors
Interaction	Whole class work, suitable for large classes

Procedure

1 This song is sung to the music of the children's song *I have a dog and my dog loves me.* Go to the Website appendix on page 149 for an on-line link to the melody. Teach the children the first verse of the song. See Box 96.

2 Ask the children what they have to do in the mornings to be clean and fresh for school. As they suggest a grooming habit, include it in the next verse of the song. Encourage the children to do actions to the song as they sing. Suggestions for actions are in Box 96.

Box 96   Morning song

Grooming habits	Song	Actions
Body	I have a body and my body is mine, I care for my body all the time.	Point to yourself.
	Body goes wobble dee dee.	Wiggle and shake your body.
Brush	I have a brush and the brush is mine, I brush my hair all the time.	Brush your hair.
	Brush goes swish swish, Body goes wobble dee dee.	Wiggle and shake your body.
Soap	I have some soap and the soap is mine, I wash my body all the time.	Wash your body.
	Soap goes rub rub,	
	Brush goes swish swish,	Brush your hair.
	Body goes wobble dee dee.	Wiggle and shake your body.

Grooming habits	Song	Actions
Water	I have some water and the water is mine, I wash my face all the time. Water goes splash splash, Soap goes rub rub, Brush goes swish swish, Body goes wobble dee dee.	Wash your face. Wash your body. Brush your hair. Wiggle and shake your body.
Toothbrush	I have a toothbrush and the toothbrush is mine, I brush my teeth all the time. Toothbrush goes up and down, Water goes splash splash, Soap goes rub rub, Brush goes swish swish, Body goes wobble dee dee.	Brush your teeth. Wash your face. Wash your body. Brush your hair. Wiggle and shake your body.

Follow-up
- Ask the children to do drawings which illustrate how they make themselves clean and fresh for school. Under each drawing, they write captions from the Actions column of Box 96, e.g. *Brush your hair*.
- For other songs, see Activities 1.5, 2.14, 6.7.

5.5 Staying clean and healthy

Level	*
Language focus	Instructions, imperative, vocabulary: parts of the body, clothes
Skills focus	Listening to a string of instructions
Thinking focus	Remembering
Teaching approach	Promote accuracy – correct errors
Interaction	Whole class work, suitable for large classes

Procedure
1 Ask the children to stand up. Read out one instruction from Box 97 and ask the children to mime the action, e.g. *Wash your face*.

2 The next time, read out two instructions, one after the other. The children listen to both instructions and then mime the actions, e.g. *Brush your hair and clean your teeth.*

3 Each time, keep adding one more item to the list of instructions. The children listen to the complete list as it gradually increases, and mime the sequence of actions in order at the end of your reading. When a child cannot remember the list, they sit down. The winner is the one who remains standing and who can remember the long list of instructions.

Box 97   Healthy habits

Wash your face	Wash your dishes
Brush your hair	Wash your clothes
Clean your teeth	Wash your glasses
Clean your shoes	Wash your socks
Wash your hair	Wash your hands

5.6 Footprints

Level	*
Language focus	Vocabulary: nouns – what we wear on our feet; verbs – what our feet can do
Skills focus	Dictionary work
Thinking focus	Selecting and investigating
Teaching approach	Promote creativity – accept errors
Interaction	Small group work
Preparation	Provide each group with a large sheet of paper, large crayons and a number of bilingual dictionaries.

Procedure

1 Tell the children to fold their large sheet of paper in half and make a line along the middle of the page (horizontally).

2 Ask one member of each group to take off his/her shoes and socks, and stand on the line on the large sheet of paper with half the feet in the top half of the paper, and half the feet in the bottom part of the paper.

3 Then one group member traces around the feet of their classmate, leaving two footprints on the line in the middle of the page.

4 Meanwhile, some group members use their dictionaries and try to fill up the top half of the paper with words which describe what we can do with our feet, leaving the footprint as an illustration in the middle of the page. See Box 98.

5 The other group members try to fill up the bottom half of the paper with the names of things we can wear on our feet. For all group members, encourage them to use their dictionaries to find the English words they want to write.

Box 98   Our feet

What can our feet do?	What can we wear on our feet?
Run	Shoes
Stand	Socks
Bounce	Boots
Jump	Skates
Kick	Skis
Walk	Football boots
Skip	Roller blades
Hop	Tennis shoes
Climb	Running shoes
Slide	Flippers
Skate	Trainers
Ski	

Follow-up
- Display the children's footprint posters in the classroom.
- You could do a similar activity, using handprints.

5.7 Doctor! Doctor!

Level	**
Language focus	Rap, vocabulary: ailments and remedies
Skills focus	Speaking: fluency, rhythm
Thinking focus	Matching
Teaching approach	Promote creativity – accept errors
Interaction	Whole class work, suitable for large classes
Preparation	Write the Doctor rap and the remedies on the board. See Box 99.

Procedure

1 Decide on a possible ailment, e.g. *My **head** is sore*. Teach the children the chant from the board, stressing the words in bold.
2 Ask the children to choose a remedy from Box 99, e.g. *go to bed*.
3 Now divide the class into two teams. One team says the part of the patient and decides on an ailment.
4 The other team says the part of the doctor. When the doctor says *This will fix it!* the children have to choose the remedy.
5 Then swap over, so everyone has a turn at being either a doctor or a patient. Make sure the children keep the flow of the chant going, stressing the words in bold.

Box 99   Doctor rap

Doctor rap	Remedies
Doctor: **One**, **two**. **How** are **you**? *Patient*: **Three**, **four**. My . . . is **sore**. *Doctor*: **Five – it**, **six – it**. **This** will **fix** it! *Patient*: **Seven**, **eight**, **nine**. I feel **fine**.	a plaster, a bandage, an aspirin, some eye drops, some cough medicine, some ear drops, some nose drops, go to bed, have a shower, have some hot tea, have some soup

---

Follow-up
- Encourage the children to create their own remedies for ailments and add these to the list.
- For other chants and raps, see Activities 1.11, 2.7, 4.4, 4.6, 5.1, 6.1.

5.8 Safety

Level	* *
Language focus	Procedure, imperative
Skills focus	Listening
Thinking focus	Sorting, inferring
Teaching approach	Promote accuracy – correct errors
Interaction	Whole class work, suitable for large classes
Preparation	On the board, write the word *SAFETY*. Underneath, write in bullet points: *Personal, Road, Sun, Water*.

Procedure

1 Remind the children about the different kinds of safety you have listed on the board. Do this in their first language if necessary.
2 Tell the children that you are going to read out some safety rules and you want them to decide if these rules apply to personal safety, road safety, sun safety, or water safety.
3 Slowly and carefully read out the first rule: *Wear a hat and a long-sleeved shirt*. Ask the children to write which area of safety this rule is addressing, e.g. *Sun safety*.
4 Then read out the other rules, and allow time for the children to write the areas of safety which match each rule.
5 Finally, check their answers.

Note: It is unlikely that the children will understand every word in the rule. However, there are enough clues for them to guess the safety area. This activity is teaching them to use their prior knowledge to predict meaning.

Box 100   Safety rules

Safety rule	Area of safety
1 Wear a hat and a long-sleeved shirt.	Sun safety
2 Look to the left (or right) and look to the right (or left) and look to the left (or right) again.	Road safety
3 Never dive into a swimming pool at the shallow end.	Water safety
4 Stop at the red light.	Road safety
5 Do not talk to strangers.	Personal safety
6 Sit in the shade.	Sun safety
7 Always tell your parents where you are going.	Personal safety
8 Do not swim immediately after eating a meal.	Water safety

Follow-up

• This activity leads nicely into a discussion about various safety rules. You could ask the children to explain why these rules are important.
• There may be other safety issues and rules that apply to your local conditions, e.g. snow safety, animal safety, home safety, playground safety. You could substitute these topics for those in Box 100.
• You could divide the class into four groups, and give each group a safety heading from the listening activity. Then they could add more rules to the list and prepare class wallcharts about various aspects of safety.

- For other procedures, see Activities 2.9, 3.4, 4.12, 4.15, 4.18, 6.10, 6.13, 6.16.

5.9 A healthy lifestyle

Level	**
Language focus	Vocabulary: weekend activities, comparatives and superlatives, *because*
Skills focus	Speaking
Thinking focus	Ranking
Teaching approach	Promote creativity – accept errors
Interaction	Pairwork, suitable for large classes
Preparation	On the board, list all the weekend activities and sentence stems from Box 101.

Procedure

1 Ask the children to read out the weekend activities from the board.
2 Ask them which activity is the healthiest and which one is the least healthy. There may be some debate about this. Let the children share their ideas, and encourage them to give reasons for their opinions, using the sentence stems from Box 101.
3 Ask the children, in pairs, to rank the activities from the least healthy to the healthiest. Again, encourage them to use the sentence stems as they discuss and debate with each other.
4 Ask the pairs to share their answers with their classmates.

Note: There are no absolute answers here, although dancing and playing basketball are obviously healthier than playing computer games. The aim of the activity is to stimulate debate and to encourage the children to give reasons for their choices.

Box 101   Weekend activities

		Sentence stems
Taking pictures with a camera	Playing the guitar	I think . . . is the healthiest activity because . . .
Dancing to music	Flying a kite	
Going shopping	Playing basketball	
Watching a video	Playing computer games	I think . . . is healthier than . . . because . . .

Follow-up

- You could conduct a class survey about weekend activities. The class could then rank their own weekend activities from the least healthy to the healthiest. The results could be recorded in a graph.
- You could ask the children to make suggestions about how to include more healthy activities in their own lifestyle.

5.10 Our feelings

Level	* *
Language focus	Verb *to be* + a complement + *when*
Skills focus	Speaking
Thinking focus	Giving examples
Teaching approach	Promote creativity – accept errors
Interaction	Group work, suitable for large classes
Preparation	Write the six feeling words on the board, along with the group questions and sentence stems. See Box 102.

Procedure

1 The children will be familiar with some of the feelings on the board, such as *happy, sad, afraid* and *sorry*. However, you may need to talk to them about feeling quiet, i.e. peaceful or reflective, and feeling strong, i.e. brave or determined.

2 Divide the class into groups with six children in each group. Allocate one of the feeling words to each child in the group. If you cannot divide your class evenly into groups of six, then allow two children to work together. For less confident learners, give them the simpler words like *sad* or *happy* and challenge your more able learners with *quiet* and *strong*.

3 Give the children a few minutes to think about circumstances when they have had these feelings.

4 Everyone in the group then takes a turn to tell the others about when they have had these feelings. For example, the group says to one member *When are you sad?* The response could be *I am sad when I see hungry children on TV.*

5 Continue until everyone in the group has had a turn to speak.

Box 102   Expressing feelings

Feeling words	Sentence stem and group questions	Sentence stem and sample answers
Afraid	*When are you* afraid?	I am afraid when I watch a scary movie.
Happy	*When are you* happy?	I am happy when I get birthday presents.
Sad	*When are you* sad?	I am sad when I see hungry children on TV.
Sorry	*When are you* sorry?	I am sorry when I hurt a friend.
Quiet	*When are you* quiet?	I am quiet when I look at the stars at night.
Strong	*When are you* strong?	I am strong when my football team does not win the game.

Follow-up

Ask the children to write sentences about each member of the group. Remind them that they now need to pay attention to the third person singular verb endings, e.g. *Tom is quiet when he **looks** at the stars at night.* The children could illustrate their sentences and display them in the classroom.

5.11 Absent from school

Level	**
Language focus	Absentee letter, vocabulary: days of the week, ailments
Skills focus	Writing
Thinking focus	Explaining
Teaching approach	Promote creativity – accept errors
Interaction	Individual work, suitable for large classes
Preparation	Make a classroom poster displaying the letter scaffolding in Box 103.

Procedure

1   Talk to the children briefly about the occasions when they have been absent from school with an illness. Tell them that they are going to write a note to their teachers explaining why they have been absent from school.

2   Refer the children to the letter scaffolding in the poster. Your less able learners will be able simply to supply one-word answers in the gaps, whereas you should encourage your more confident learners to expand on their reasons for being absent.

3   When they have finished, get the children to swap their writing with a classmate. Ask them to read the letter and make suggestions to their partner about ways to improve their writing, e.g. they may observe errors in spelling, grammar, vocabulary or punctuation, or they may suggest some additional ideas.

Box 103   Absentee letter scaffolding

Date: . . . .
Dear . . . .
I'm sorry I was absent from school on . . . . (When? Which day?)
I had . . . . (A toothache? A stomach ache?)
Your student
. . . . (Your name)

Follow-up

• When children are absent from school in the future, refer them to the absentee letter scaffolding poster and ask them to write you an absentee note.

• For other cards, letters and emails, see Activities 2.12, 4.8, 5.15, 6.8.

5.12 Unhealthy activities

Level	**
Language focus	Past continuous and simple present tense, vocabulary: ailments
Skills focus	Reading
Thinking focus	Locating and matching
Teaching approach	Promote accuracy – correct errors
Interaction	Whole class work
Preparation	Photocopy the sentence strips from Box 104. You will probably have to make a few copies. Cut the sentences up into individual sentence strips.

Procedure

1 Jumble the sentence strips and distribute them around the class: one sentence strip for each child.

2 Tell the children that some of them will have an unhealthy activity, and others will have the results or consequences of this activity.

3 Each child then silently reads his/her own sentence strip and circulates around the room to find a partner with a matching sentence strip, i.e. they match an unhealthy activity to a consequence.

4 When they think they have a match, they read out the activity and the consequence to the class.

Box 104   Unhealthy activities and their consequences

Sentence strips: unhealthy activities	Sentence strips: consequences
Yesterday I was listening to loud CDs all day.	Today I have an earache.
Yesterday I was swimming in the hot sun all day.	Today I have sunburn.
Yesterday I was eating chips all day.	Today I have a stomach ache.
Yesterday I was crunching sweets all day.	Today I have a toothache.
Yesterday I was playing in the snow all day.	Today I have a cold.
Yesterday I was playing football all day.	Today I have sore legs.
Yesterday I was watching TV all day.	Today I have sore eyes.
Yesterday I was singing loudly all day.	Today I have a sore throat.

© Cambridge University Press 2007

5.13 The senses

Level	* * *
Language focus	Vocabulary: parts of the body, sensing verbs, appraisal adjectives
Skills focus	Speaking
Thinking focus	Inventing
Teaching approach	Promote creativity – accept errors
Interaction	Group work, suitable for large classes
Preparation	Write the parts of the body on the board, along with the senses. Make sure you jumble the words in the senses column, so that the children can match them to the body part later. Write the sentence stems on the board. See Box 105.

Procedure

1 Divide the class into small groups with five children in each group. Their first task is to match the body part to the sense.

2 Then ask each child to choose one of the senses. Ask the children to think about a pleasant experience and an unpleasant experience when they have used this sense. Some sample answers are in Box 105.

3 Finally, each member shares his/her experience with the group, using the sentence stems from Box 105, e.g. *Once I saw a flower. It was beautiful.*

Box 105   Experiencing the senses

Body parts	Senses	Sentence stems	Pleasant experiences: sample answers	Unpleasant experiences: sample answers
eye	see	Once I saw . . . It was . . .	flower/beautiful	face/unfriendly
nose	smell	Once I smelt . . . It was . . .	food/delicious	fish/dead
ear	hear	Once I heard . . . It was . . .	music/lovely	alarm clock/loud
tongue	taste	Once I tasted . . . It was . . .	ice cream/sweet	lemon/sour
finger	touch	Once I touched . . . It was . . .	cat/soft	cooker/hot

5.14 An accident

Level	* * *
Language focus	Recount, vocabulary: medical, time-sequencing signals
Skills focus	Reading and speaking
Thinking focus	Sequencing, cause and effect
Teaching approach	Promote accuracy – correct errors
Interaction	Pairwork, suitable for large classes
Preparation	Write the random vocabulary on the board from Box 106. Write some of the time-sequencing signals from the activity on the board, e.g. *First, then, next, after that, finally.*

Procedure

1 Ask the children to read the random vocabulary from Box 106.
2 Divide the class into pairs and ask them to order the words into an accident timeline. Encourage the children to use time-sequencing signals, e.g. *What happened first? What happened next? What happened after that?*
3 Call on pairs to share their answers with the class, using time-sequencing signals.

Box 106   Accident timeline

Random vocabulary	Answers
chemist, broken leg, doctor, ambulance, accident, aspirin, foggy weather, hospital	foggy weather – accident – broken leg – ambulance – hospital – doctor – chemist – aspirin

---

Follow-up

• The children could write a short recount about an accident, following the timeline in the activity.
• Children could create other random vocabulary boxes about a sporting accident or a fire and challenge their classmates to arrange the words in order.
• For other factual recounts, see Activities 1.17, 4.16.

5.15 Get well card

Level	* * *
Language focus	Get well card
Skills focus	Writing
Thinking focus	Constructing
Teaching approach	Promote accuracy – correct errors
Interaction	Individual work, suitable for large classes
Preparation	Make a wall poster based on the template in Box 107.

Procedure

1 Talk to the children about the role of get well cards in encouraging their friends when they are away from school because of illness.
2 Show the class the wall poster template. Ask the children to suggest ideas for completing the sentence stems and write their suggestions on the board. Some models are in Box 107.
3 Then jointly construct a model get well card by choosing from the children's suggestions.

Note: When you construct a text jointly, you ask the children to suggest what you should write and then record their suggestions on the board. Then you ask the others to comment on ways to improve the text by either correcting errors or adding more ideas.

Follow-up
• The next time one of the children is absent because of illness, ask the children to make get well cards and send them home. They are sure to brighten the day for someone who is not feeling very well.
• For other cards, letters and emails, see Activities 2.12, 4.8, 5.11, 6.8.

Box 107   Get well card template

Date ....

Dear ....

We are sorry to hear that/about .....
....
....
....

We all miss you and we hope that ....
....
....
....

Best wishes from your friends at ....
....
....

(name of the school)

Get well card models

We are sorry to hear that:
- you have a cold.
- you have a stomach ache.
- you have a headache.

We are sorry to hear about:
- your broken arm/leg.
- your accident.

We hope that:
- you will be better soon.
- you will be back at school soon.
- you will be out of hospital soon.

© Cambridge University Press 2007

5.16 Personal affirmations

Level	* * *
Language focus	Descriptions: personal attributes, skills, physical appearance
Skills focus	Writing
Thinking focus	Creating
Teaching approach	Promote creativity – accept errors
Interaction	Whole class work, suitable for large classes
Preparation	On the board, write the sentence stems from the headings in Box 108.

Procedure

1 Tell the children that when we are positive and kind to each other, we help to create healthy relationships in the class. Ask them to think about things they could say to affirm their classmates.

2 Each child starts with a blank piece of paper with his/her name at the top.

3 They pass their paper to the right and this person writes one affirmation, using the sentence stems from the board. They should start with a positive statement about physical appearance, making sure to include descriptive adjectives. Some examples are in Box 108.

4 They then pass the paper to the next person on the right. This time, the children write a positive personal attribute for the person whose name appears at the top of the page.

5 The paper is passed for a third time, and the children write about a skill of the person whose name appears at the top of the paper.

6 Finally, the paper is returned to the original owner who is able to read the kind affirmations of his/her classmates.

Follow-up

The children could keep their personal affirmations, or they could be displayed in the classroom. Over time, the children could add other positive statements about their classmates.

Box 108   Personal descriptions

Physical descriptions sentence stems: You have . . . You are . . .	Personal attributes sentence stem: You are a/an . . . person.	Skills sentence stem: You can . . .
You have beautiful, clean hair. You have lovely, big, dark eyes. You have nice, small, soft hands. You have strong, straight legs. You have beautiful, straight, white teeth. You are tall and thin. You are small and strong.	clever excellent friendly good happy interesting kind quiet helpful	catch, throw, hit, kick a ball very well draw, paint, colour pictures very well study, learn, read, speak, sing very well run, swim, climb, dance, skate, ski very quickly / very well

---

5.17 Healthy and unhealthy foods

Level	* * *
Language focus	Graph, comparatives and superlatives
Skills focus	Writing
Thinking focus	Analysing
Teaching approach	Promote creativity – accept errors
Interaction	Pairwork, suitable for large classes
Preparation	Draw the graph on the board. Write the sentence stems from Box 109.

Procedure

1 Direct the children to the graph on the board. Point out that one shade represents the weekly eating habits of Ann and the other shade represents the weekly eating habits of Sally.
2 Now refer to the sentence stems and together try to complete a few examples.
3 Finally, ask the children to write one sentence about the graph.
4 When they have finished, ask them to exchange their work with a partner. Encourage them to proofread the sentence and make suggestions about how to improve the text.

Box 109   Eating habits

Graph	Sentence stems
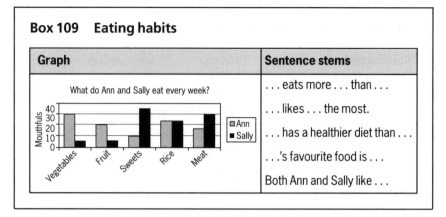	. . . eats more . . . than . . . . . . likes . . . the most. . . . has a healthier diet than . . . . . .'s favourite food is . . . Both Ann and Sally like . . .

Follow-up
- Ask the children, in pairs, to draw a graph of their own eating habits and write sentences describing their graphs. Display the graphs and the explanations in the classroom.
- For other graphs and diagrams, see Activities 3.9, 4.13, 5.18, 6.15.

5.18 Food pyramid

Level	* * *
Language focus	Diagram, vocabulary: food
Skills focus	Listening for details, spelling
Thinking focus	Sorting information
Teaching approach	Promote accuracy – correct errors
Interaction	Pairwork, suitable for large classes
Preparation	Draw the food pyramid on the board. See Box 110.

Procedure

1 Refer to the food pyramid on the board and give one example of the kinds of foods that belong in each section of the pyramid.
2 Tell the children to copy the pyramid, allowing enough room to write in food types.
3 Read from the list of foods in Box 110, choosing food items from different categories each time. Allow the children time to think about where to write the food in the pyramid.
4 When you have finished, ask the children to check their answers with a partner.

Box 110   Diagram: food pyramid

Food pyramid	Foods to categorise
	Sugar: biscuit, cake, chocolate, jam, lemonade, sweets *Dairy, meat, eggs:* butter, cheese, chicken, fish, milk, sausage *Fruit and vegetables:* apple, banana, bean, carrot, coconut, lemon, lime, mango, onion, orange, pea, pear, pineapple, potato, tomato, watermelon *Cereals:* bread, flour, pasta, rice

Follow-up
- From this activity, children could analyse what kinds of food they eat. Is their diet made up of mainly cereals and fresh fruit and vegetables? Do they eat too many sweet foods?
- Perhaps there are foods that the children would like to add to the pyramid, but they do not know the English word. This is an ideal opportunity to expand their vocabulary, keeping in mind that some foods are a combination of food types, e.g. *soup, hamburger* or *sandwich*.
- For other graphs and diagrams, see Activities 3.9, 4.13, 5.17, 6.15.

6 About me

6.1 My family

Level	*
Language focus	Vocabulary: family members, adjectives
Skills focus	Listening for details, pronunciation: stress and rhythm
Thinking focus	Recalling
Teaching approach	Promote accuracy – correct errors
Interaction	Whole class work, suitable for large classes

Note: Do not write the chant on the board. You want the children to listen carefully and repeat the chant and copy the hand movements.

Procedure

1 Ask the children to stand up and shake their hands. This is to loosen up their finger muscles for a finger play. Finger plays not only tap into a kinaesthetic style of learning, but also help to develop the children's fine motor skills.

2 Tell them that you are going to teach them a finger play about families.

3 Read out the first line of the finger play and demonstrate the accompanying actions. See Box 111.

4 The children repeat the first line with the actions. The stressed syllables are in bold.

5 Check pronunciation, stress and rhythm. Pay attention to the schwa / ə / sound on the weak syllables.

6 Now read out lines 2 and 3 and ask the children to listen and repeat while following your hand actions.

7 Repeat lines 1, 2 and 3 until you are satisfied that the children are saying the chant correctly and doing the hand actions.

8 Now introduce lines 4, 5 and 6 and ask the children to repeat and copy the hand actions.

9 Finally, perform the complete finger play together.

Box 111 Family finger play

Finger play: chant	Finger play: hand movements
1 **Mother** and **father** **stand**ing **tall**. 2 **Brother** is **big**, 3 and **sister** is **small**. 4 **Where** is the **baby**? **Where** is the **baby**? 5 **Wah! Wah! Wah!** 6 I **hear** him/her **call**!	1 Show the index fingers first and then the middle fingers. Use both hands. Hold the other fingers down with the thumb. 2 Show the ring fingers on both hands, along with the index and middle fingers. 3 Show the little fingers. Now all fingers are showing, but the thumbs are hidden. 4 Close hands into a fist and wiggle both thumbs. 5 and **6** Put both hands over your ears.

Follow-up

There are many well-known activities which not only promote language learning, but also assist with the development of fine motor and gross motor skills, e.g. Simon says.

6.2 My classroom

Level	*
Language focus	Vocabulary: classroom objects
Skills focus	Listening for details
Thinking focus	Following directions
Teaching approach	Promote accuracy – correct errors
Interaction	Whole class work, suitable for large classes
Preparation	On small slips of paper, write the names of a number of familiar classroom items. Choose objects from the basic game. See Box 112. Jumble these and put them into a container.

Procedure

1 Ask each child to choose one object from the classroom and place it on his/her desk.

2 Then ask the children to stand and listen to the names of the objects as you draw them out of the container.

3 As you select a slip of paper, read out the name of the object. Anyone with this object has to sit down.

4 Continue to draw out all the slips of paper one by one, and read out the name of the object. The last children left standing are the winners.

5 It is possible that some children have chosen objects which you did not include in your list. If they know the English word for these items, then they win bonus points.

Box 112   Classroom objects

Classroom objects: basic game	Classroom objects: advanced game
Book	*Add one adjective:*
Pen	Red pencil
Picture	Old toy
Eraser	Tennis ball
Pencil	*Add two adjectives:*
Ruler	New English book
Ball	Big picture book
Game	Old test book
Toy	
Bag	
Box	

Follow-up

As the children become familiar with this game, they will grow more adventurous in their choice of objects. They will be motivated to check vocabulary in their dictionaries and choose unusual items in order to outsmart you. At this stage, you could choose items from the 'advanced game' column. Give them some warning that you will be playing the game in the near future, and this should add to their excitement and determination to be the last one standing.

6.3 My home

Level	*
Language focus	Vocabulary: ordinal numbers and household items
Skills focus	Listening for details, spelling
Thinking focus	Identifying
Teaching approach	Promote accuracy – correct errors
Interaction	Whole class work, suitable for large classes

Procedure

1 Tell the children that you are going to read out the names of some household items. You want them to write some of these words – but not all of them.

2 Tell the children that you want them to write the third word in your list. See the example in Box 113. Then read out the example words from the household list and check their answers.

3 Continue to read out the lists of words, giving the children time to write as you read. Make sure they understand that you do not want them to write all the words in the list, but only the ones you have indicated at the beginning, e.g. *Write the second and fifth words.*

4 Each time, the task becomes more difficult. This is a chance for you to identify the children's strengths and weaknesses in listening and spelling.

Box 113 Household items

Ordinal number clue	Household list
Example: Write the third word.	**Example:** clock, TV, **chair**
Write the second and fifth words.	phone, **cupboard**, mat, lamp, **bath**
Write the second, fourth and fifth words.	bed, **armchair**, garden, **mirror**, **bookcase**, table
Write the third, sixth, seventh and ninth words.	camera, lamp, **radio**, bed, phone, **sofa**, **window**, chair, **door**, bath
Write the second, fourth, fifth, eighth and tenth words.	mat, **garden**, bookcase, **TV**, **clock**, bed, door, **table**, camera, **box**

Follow-up

This activity can be adapted to include any vocabulary that you want to revise.

6.4 My school books

Level	*
Language focus	Label, vocabulary: classroom book labelling
Skills focus	Reading and writing
Thinking focus	Recalling and naming
Teaching approach	Promote creativity – accept errors
Interaction	Whole class work, suitable for large classes
Preparation	If you have time, create label templates on your computer and print them onto sticky paper. Otherwise, simply write the label template on the board. See Box 114.

Procedure

1 Tell the children that they are going to create personalised labels for their English exercise books.

2 Draw their attention to the six headings in the label template. See Box 114. Make sure they know the meaning of each of these headings.

3 Ask the children to complete the template with their own details.

Box 114   Label template

Label template	Completed label
Name: . . . . **Address:**	**Name:** Tom Green **Address:** 9 Station Road, Summerville.
Class: . . . . **Classroom:** . . . . **Teacher:** . . . . **School:**	**Class:** English **Classroom:** Room 4E **Teacher:** Mrs Brown **School:** Happy Street Primary School

---

Follow-up

• The children decorate their labels with pictures, e.g. their favourite pop group or football star.

• They could make more labels for their other subjects, so that all their class exercise books have an English label.

6.5 My free time

Level	*
Language focus	Present continuous tense
Skills focus	Speaking: pronunciation
Thinking focus	Identifying and memorising
Teaching approach	Promote accuracy – correct errors
Interaction	Small group work, suitable for large classes

Procedure

1 Divide the class into groups of three. Each person in the group has to decide on three free time activities.

2 The first person mimes the three activities and then says *What am I doing?*

3 The others have to guess the three activities and name them in the correct order. In giving their answers, they say *You are . . . -ing . . .* See Box 115 for some examples.

4 Then the others in the group have a turn at miming while their classmates try to guess the three activities in the correct order.

5 While the children are miming and guessing, go from group to group and check their pronunciation and grammar.

Box 115   Free time activities

You are: watching TV, playing computer games, riding your bike, kicking a football, playing badminton, reading a book, hitting a baseball, catching a basketball, playing with a doll, swimming in a pool, drawing a picture, singing a song, taking a photo with your camera, fishing, playing a guitar, listening to a CD, playing the piano

---

Follow-up
Rather than miming the free time activities, the children could draw them. The others in the group have to guess the activities from the drawings. You could give a time limit to add to the excitement of the game.

6.6 My mum's mobile phone

Level	*
Language focus	Text messages, the alphabet, numbers, questions
Skills focus	Writing: punctuation
Thinking focus	Analysing and discovering
Teaching approach	Promote creativity – accept errors
Interaction	Pairwork
Preparation	Write the example text message on the board. See Box 116.

Procedure

1 Some children will be familiar with text messaging and the short cuts that mobile phone users often use. For the others, tell them that, to save money, people shorten their text messages and use symbols instead of whole words.

2 Refer the class to the example text message on the board. Ask them to solve the puzzle and read out the text message. Write the example out in full. See Box 116.

3 Write another message on the board. See the text messages puzzles in Box 116.

4 Ask the children, in pairs, to solve the puzzle of this text message. Ask them to write the message out in full.

5 Call on pairs to share their answers with the class.

Box 116 Text messages

Text messages: puzzles	Text messages: answers
Example: Can U come 4 T? What R U eating 4 T? Ps. R U watching TV? Can U C me on TV?	**Example:** Can you come for tea? What are you eating for tea? Peas. Are you watching TV? Can you see me on TV?
How many letters R there? There R 2 4 U and 1 4 me.	How many letters are there? There are two for you and one for me.

Follow-up

• Continue with the other text message puzzles from Box 116.

• Ask the children, in pairs, to devise their own text messages using symbols. They could then 'send' their text message on a piece of paper and challenge their partner to solve their text message puzzle. Then the classmate writes another text message in reply.

6.7 My friends

Level	* *
Language focus	Song, vocabulary: adjectives describing personal attributes, leisure activities
Skills focus	Speaking: fluency and rhythm
Thinking focus	Inventing
Teaching approach	Promote creativity – accept errors
Interaction	Whole class work, suitable for large classes
Preparation	On the board, write the adjectives describing personal attributes and leisure activities. See Box 117. Prepare a transparency of the song.

Procedure

1 Show the children the transparency of *The friendship song* in Box 117 and sing the song to them. The tune is *Edelweiss* from the film *The Sound of Music*. See the Website appendix on page 149 for an on-line link to the melody.

2 Choose a name from the class and insert it instead of the name in the sample song. Write the new name onto the transparency.

3 As a class, decide on four personal descriptions of this person and insert them into the song.

4 Now include one of this person's leisure-time activities in the song.

5 Finally, sing the new song together.

Box 117   The friendship song

The friendship song	Adjectives: personal attributes	Leisure activities
Jacky Chan, Jacky Chan, We are happy to know you. **Friendly and kind,** **Gentle and wise,** We are lucky to know you. **Reader of books**, may you grow and learn, Grow and learn forever. **Jacky Chan, Jacky Chan,** Let us be friends forever.	good, gentle, small, lucky, tall, helpful, young, sweet, smart, neat, clever, tidy, kind, bright, short, quick, happy, friendly, wise, nice, thoughtful, polite	Learner of: art, sport, dance, music, English Player of: flute, piano, tennis, music, games Reader of: books, comics, stories Watcher of: films

© Cambridge University Press 2007

Follow-up
- When the children can confidently sing the song, get them to write a version about one of their friends. They may want to do this in pairs or small groups. Then ask them to perform their song for the class.
- For other songs, see Activities 1.5, 2.14, 5.4.

6.8 My birthday party

Level	**
Language focus	Invitation, interrogatives and modals
Skills focus	Reading: language in context
Thinking focus	Predicting
Teaching approach	Promote accuracy – correct errors
Interaction	Whole class work, suitable for large classes
Preparation	Write the whole text onto a transparency or large poster. Have some small pieces of sticky paper handy to cover some of the words.

Procedure
1 Together read the birthday invitation.
2 Jointly construct the details for the gaps, e.g. the date of the party. Write these into the invitation.
3 Using pieces of sticky paper, cover the words *would, when, where, can.* These are the key words you want to focus on in this activity.
4 Now, as a class, start to read the invitation again. Choose children to give the missing words, all the time encouraging discussion about why this word would be most suitable. When the word has been correctly identified, remove the sticky paper and read the text together.

Follow-up
- This activity is called a 'progressive cloze'. You can use this technique with any short text. Progressively cover more and more words in the text. Choose words that you want to focus on in your teaching. These may be verbs like *is*, prepositions such as *on*, or new vocabulary.
- Encourage the children to create their own birthday invitations and decorate them.
- Display the birthday invitation template in the classroom, so that the children can use it for their own invitations.
- For other cards, letters and emails, see Activities 2.12, 4.8, 5.11, 5.15.

Box 118   A birthday invitation

Dear . . . .

Would you like to come to my birthday party on . . . . (Date)?

When does the party start? . . . .

Where is the party? . . . .

Please tick here if you can come. ☐

© Cambridge University Press 2007

6.9 My school excursion

Level	**
Language focus	Announcement, question words
Skills focus	Listening for details, note taking
Thinking focus	Discriminating
Teaching approach	Promote accuracy – correct errors
Interaction	Pairwork, suitable for large classes
Preparation	Write the note-taking grid on the board. See Box 119.

Procedure

1 Tell the children that the school principal is going to read out an important announcement about an excursion and they will have to note some specific details.
2 Ask the children, in pairs, to copy the note-taking grid from the board.
3 Slowly and carefully, read out the announcement. Make your voice sound authoritative, so that the children get the sense that the school principal is delivering the message.
4 Ask the pairs to check their answers and make changes if they think they need to.
5 Call on the children to give their answers, and complete the note-taking grid on the board.

Box 119   Excursion announcement

The principal's excursion announcement	Note-taking grid
Good morning, everyone. Next Wednesday we will all go to the zoo. We will take the bus and I want you to meet in the playground at 9 am. Please bring a bottle of water, a sandwich and some fruit. And don't forget to wear a hat. It will be quite a hot day. Thank you, children.	**When? Day** . . . . **Time** . . . . **Where?** . . . . **Meet?** . . . . **Bring?** . . . . **Wear?** . . . .

Follow-up
- For future excursions or other school functions, use this activity to give the announcement and ask the children to note the details.
- School excursions also provide an excellent opportunity for both oral and written recounts.
- For other factual recounts, see Activities 1.17, 4.16, 5.14.

6.10 My sporting skills

Level	**
Language focus	Procedure, imperative
Skills focus	Writing
Thinking focus	Creating
Teaching approach	Promote creativity – accept errors
Interaction	Pairwork, suitable for large classes
Preparation	Write the sample procedure on a transparency. See Box 120.

Procedure
1 Divide the class into pairs. Try to match children with similar sporting interests.
2 Ask the children to think about one specific skill they need in order to be successful in their sport. It could be how to hold a bat, how to serve in tennis, or how to dive into a pool. For those who do not play a sport, encourage them to choose leisure activities like how to bait a fishing hook, or musical skills like how to hold a violin.
3 Show the children the sample procedure from Box 120 and read it together.
4 Ask the children to write four or five steps to describe a skill to a Martian. They should keep their sentences short and begin each sentence with the imperative form of the verb.
5 Select children to read out their instructions to their classmates.

Box 120   How to catch a ball

1 Watch the ball.
2 Bend your knees.
3 Hold up two hands next to your chest.
4 Watch the ball all the way into your hands.
5 Use both hands to catch the ball.

© Cambridge University Press 2007

Follow-up

- The children's procedures could be decorated with pictures to illustrate the instructions and then be displayed in the classroom.
- For other procedures and instructions, see Activities 2.9, 3.4, 4.12, 4.15, 4.18, 5.8, 6.13, 6.16.

6.11   My favourite TV show

Level	**
Language focus	Survey, interrogatives
Skills focus	Speaking: accuracy and fluency, listening for details
Thinking focus	Giving examples
Teaching approach	Promote accuracy – correct errors
Interaction	Pairwork, suitable for large classes
Preparation	Photocopy the survey questions and the sentence stems from Box 121.

Procedure

1 Divide the class into pairs and provide each pair with a copy of the survey form. See Box 121.
2 Ask one person to start asking the questions in the survey and filling in the answers.

3   Encourage the person giving the answers to use the sentence stems in the handout.

4   Circulate among the pairs, checking on accuracy and fluency.

5   If you have time, get the pairs to swap roles.

Box 121   TV survey form

TV survey questions	Survey answers: sentence stems
1 What is your favourite TV show?	**1** My favourite TV show is . . .
2 When is it on TV?	**2** It's on TV on . . .
3 When does it start?	**3** It starts at . . .
4 What channel is it on?	**4** It's on channel . . .
5 How often do you watch it?	**5** I watch it every . . .
6 Why do you like it?	**6** I like it because . . .

© Cambridge University Press 2007

Follow-up

• Ask the children to give feedback about their partner to the whole class. Draw their attention to the change from the first person to the third person, and make sure they pronounce the third person singular *s* when they say the verbs, e.g. *She watches it every Monday.*

• The children mingle in the classroom and ask five others about their viewing habits. They could then report their findings to the class, e.g. *Four out of five children watch . . . They watch it every . . . They like it because . . .*

• Make graphs which represent the viewing habits of the class. Ask the children to write about the graphs. For an example of how to describe a graph, see Activity 5.17.

6.12 My favourite party game

Level	**
Language focus	Description, relative pronoun, adverbs of time
Skills focus	Reading
Thinking focus	Locating and matching
Teaching approach	Promote accuracy – correct errors
Interaction	Whole class work
Preparation	Start with a small prize. It could be a notebook or a coloured pen. Wrap it in newspaper and glue one of the sentence clues onto the parcel. See Box 122. Wrap it again and glue on another sentence clue. Keep going until you have a very large parcel with one sentence clue glued on the top. You could wrap this last layer with coloured paper.

Procedure

1 Ask one of the children to read out the first sentence clue and then he/she gives the parcel to someone in the class.
2 This child takes off one layer of paper and reads out the next clue. He/She then decides who should receive the parcel next.
3 Each time that the parcel is passed, the child unwraps one layer of paper, reads out the clue to the class, and then passes the parcel to another child.
4 The child who unwraps the last layer can keep the prize.

Box 122   Pass the parcel

Sentence clue: Pass the parcel to the boy/girl/person who . . .	Sentence clue: Pass the parcel to the boy/girl/person who . . .	Sentence clue: Pass the parcel to the boy/girl/person who . . .
– is sitting next to the door. – is wearing glasses. – is learning how to swim. – is standing up.	– likes singing. – enjoys playing basketball. – likes eating bananas. – enjoys going to parties.	– always talks in class. – always listens to the teacher. – never forgets to do his/her homework. – always helps others.

Follow-up
The children could make their own parcels and write their own clues. Store these in the classroom. They could then play the party game as a warm-up activity or as a reward for hard work.

6.13 My computer class

Level	* * *
Language focus	Instructions, prepositions, vocabulary: computer
Skills focus	Listening for details
Thinking focus	Discriminating
Teaching approach	Promote accuracy – correct errors
Interaction	Pairwork, suitable for large classes
Preparation	On the board, write the missing words from Box 123.

Procedure

1 Many children already have computer skills, so you could briefly ask them to tell you some of the things they can do with their computers.

2 Ask the children to write numbers *1* to *8* on a piece of paper, leaving room to write in the missing words.

3 Tell them that you are going to read out some instructions for using their computer. You want them to choose from the words on the board in order to complete the instructions. If you think your children can cope without the words on the board, then allow them to listen and complete the cloze activity without any prompts.

4 Now read out the instructions at a steady pace. When you get to the first gap in the cloze exercise, say *Buzz*. This will indicate to the children that there is a gap in the sentence. Then say *Number 1*. Allow time for the children to write the missing word next to their number 1.

5 Then continue reading. When you get to the next gap, say *Buzz*. Then say *Number 2*. Next to their number 2, they write the missing word.

6 Continue reading until you have completed the exercise.

7 Ask the children, in pairs, to compare their answers while you read the cloze activity again.

Box 123 Computer instructions

Computer instructions cloze activity	Computer instructions cloze answers
– To **(1)** . . . . a new file, click **(2)** . . . . the icon. – **(3)** . . . . your work **(4)** . . . . you turn off your computer. – Cut the picture from the file and **(5)** . . . . it **(6)** . . . . your sentence. – Do a spell check **(7)** . . . . you send the **(8)**	– To **open** a new file, click **on** the icon. – **Save** your work **before** you turn off your computer. – Cut the picture from the file and **paste** it **below** your sentence. – Do a spell check **before** you send the **email**.
<u>Missing words</u>: before, before, on, below, save, open, email, paste	

Follow-up
- On the board, write any new vocabulary from the cloze, and provide the meaning of these words in the children's first language. Then ask them to write some more instructions describing what they can do on the computer, e.g. how to do a web search. Once more, provide the English words that the children need to write their instructions.
- For other procedures and instructions, see Activities 2.9, 3.4, 4.12, 4.15, 4.18, 5.8, 6.10, 6.16.

6.14 My mathematics class

Level	* * *
Language focus	Mathematics word problem, vocabulary: days of the week
Skills focus	Reading for gist and details
Thinking focus	Problem solving
Teaching approach	Promote accuracy – correct errors
Interaction	Pairwork, suitable for large classes
Preparation	Write a word problem on the board. See Box 124.

Note: The focus of this activity is to read and comprehend. Mathematics is simply the context for the text.

Procedure

1 Divide the class into pairs and ask the children to read the word problem. They may not know all the vocabulary, but they should get the gist of the text.

2 Then ask them, in pairs, to translate this word problem into a number problem. See Box 124. Encourage the pairs to talk together as they solve the problem.

3 Call on the children to share their answers with the class.

Box 124   Mathematics problems

Word problem	Number problem
Every day, William plays marbles with his friends. On Monday, Tuesday, Wednesday and Thursday William won five marbles each day. On Friday he lost eight marbles. How many marbles did he win?	$(4 \times 5) - 8 = 12$
Jill is learning to play the piano. She has two lessons every week. On Mondays and Fridays she practises in the mornings and in the afternoons. On Wednesdays, Tuesdays and Thursdays she practises in the mornings. How many times does Jill play the piano each week?	$2 + (2 \times 2) + 3 = 9$

Follow-up

Ask the children to create other word problems to challenge their classmates. They should write their name on a piece of paper and then write a word problem, e.g. about chickens laying eggs in the farmyard, or about children travelling on the school bus. Collect all the word problems and hand them out to everyone in the class. When the children think they have written the correct number problem, they should go to the original author and check their answer. Encourage the children to use this opportunity to recycle vocabulary, and to use their dictionaries to include new words in their word problems.

6.15 My science class

Level	***
Language focus	Diagram, explanation, simple present tense, time markers
Skills focus	Listening for details
Thinking focus	Following directions, interpreting
Teaching approach	Promote accuracy – correct errors
Interaction	Individual work, suitable for large classes
Preparation	Draw the life cycle template on the board. In the centre, write *The life cycle of a frog*, but leave the other circles blank. See Box 125.

Procedure

1 Tell the children that you are going to read an explanation about the life cycle of a frog. See Box 126.
2 Ask them to copy the blank template of the life cycle of a frog, filling in only the central circle *The life cycle of a frog*. See Box 125.
3 As you read the explanation, ask them to draw what they hear in the life cycle diagram. They should draw their pictures in the circles.
4 Check their drawings and display them in the class.

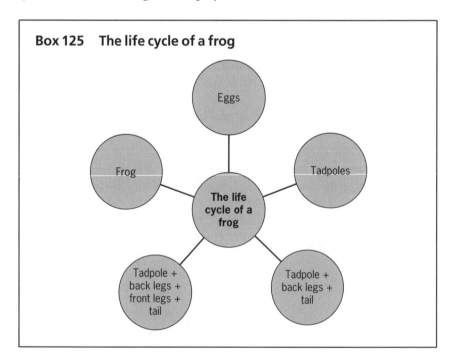

Box 125   The life cycle of a frog

Eggs

Frog

Tadpoles

The life cycle of a frog

Tadpole + back legs + front legs + tail

Tadpole + back legs + tail

Box 126   Explanation: How do frogs reproduce?

First, the female frog lays her eggs. Then small tadpoles hatch from the eggs. A tadpole looks like an egg with a tail. Next, the tadpole grows back legs. Then the tadpole grows front legs, but it still has a tail. Finally, the tadpole loses its tail and becomes a frog. It can leave the water and hop onto some rocks.

Follow-up

- You could use other cycles for this activity, such as the life cycle of a butterfly or the rain cycle.
- For other graphs and diagrams, see Activities 3.9, 4.13, 5.17, 5.18.

6.16 My social education class

Level	* * *
Language focus	Making suggestions, modal verbs, conjunctions
Skills focus	Speaking
Thinking focus	Creating
Teaching approach	Promote creativity – accept errors
Interaction	Group work, suitable for large classes
Preparation	On the board, write the words *Reduce, Reuse, Recycle*. Then write the sentence stems from Box 127.

Procedure

1   Remind the class that everybody should play a part in protecting the environment and one way to help is through limiting the amount of rubbish we generate at school and at home.
2   Direct their attention to the three words on the board (*Reduce*, *Reuse* and *Recycle*) and explain these terms in their first language.
3   Tell the children that you want them to come up with suggestions about how they could implement these environmental principles at home and at school.
4   Divide the class into three groups. Allocate one of the words on the board to each group. If you have a large class, divide the children into six or nine groups, and divide the words on the board between the groups.
5   Now ask the children to use the sentence stems to make suggestions about how to reduce, reuse or recycle waste. See Box 127 for some ideas. Encourage each person in the group to make a suggestion.
6   Mingle among the groups and offer praise and other suggestions.

Box 127　Reduce, reuse, recycle

Sentence stems	Suggestions
At home we could . . . At home we should . . . At school we could . . . At school we should . . .	**Reduce:** – take our own shopping bags to the supermarket – buy goods with little or no packaging – say *No* to plastic bags **Reuse:** – start a compost for food scraps – use magazines and paper for school craft activities – give our old games and clothes to charity **Recycle:** – collect bottles, cans, and paper, cardboard and plastic containers and put them into recycling bins

Follow-up
- Ask each group to tell the class about their suggestions. Each group could record their suggestions on a piece of card and display them in the classroom.
- Here is another activity that might be a useful preparation for the above activity. Read out a list of items and ask the children to write them down in the appropriate recycling 'bin'. The bins are labelled: *paper, plastic, glass, food scraps, aluminium cans*. The list of items that are read out could include things like: *a bottle, a banana skin, a newspaper, a yoghurt pot, a drink can*.
- The children could create posters to promote environmentally friendly practices at their school. These could be displayed on notice boards throughout the school.
- For other procedures and instructions, see Activities 2.9, 3.4, 4.12, 4.15, 4.18, 5.8, 6.10, 6.13.

6.17 My poetry class

Level	* * *
Language focus	Poem: cinquain, syllables, adjectives, verbs, adverbs
Skills focus	Writing
Thinking focus	Creating
Teaching approach	Promote creativity – accept errors
Interaction	Individual work, suitable for large classes
Preparation	Write the model cinquain on the board. See Box 128.

Procedure

1 Using the cinquain template as a guide, explain the formula for writing a cinquain. Refer to the model on the board. See Box 128.

2 Make sure the children understand that each line is limited by a number of syllables. Count these syllables together. If you think this is too difficult, you could structure the cinquain according to a number of words, rather than a number of syllables.

3 Ask the children to write a cinquain about their best friend.

Box 128   Cinquain

Cinquain template	Syllables	Model cinquain
Line 1: Name of a friend	2 syllables	Sally
Line 2: Adjectives describing your friend	4 syllables	Sure, strong, honest
Line 3: Verbs which apply to your friend	6 syllables	Learn, think, ride, walk, listen
Line 4: Adverbs which apply to your friend	8 syllables	Here, near, together, quietly
Line 5: Similar word to line 1	2 syllables	Best friend

Follow-up

* The children make friendship cards. They write their cinquain onto a card and decorate it and then give the card to a friend.
* Cinquains can be written about any topic. You could choose an animal, e.g. spider; food, e.g. ice cream; a relative, e.g. sister; a sport, e.g. tennis; an aspect of nature, e.g. jungle; the weather, e.g. rainbow. Every time you want to revise some aspect of vocabulary, you could use this activity.
* For other poems and tongue twisters, see Activities 1.6, 4.5.

6.18 My music class

Level	* * *
Language focus	Narrative, simple present, present continuous
Skills focus	Writing
Thinking focus	Creating
Teaching approach	Promote creativity – accept errors
Interaction	Pairwork, suitable for large classes
Preparation	You will need a recording of 'In the Hall of the Mountain King' from *Peer Gynt* by Grieg. On the board, write the sentence stems from Box 129.

Procedure

1 Tell the children that you are going to play some music. This music describes the adventures of Peer Gynt (a little boy), a giant Mountain King, and the king's trolls. You may need to explain the meaning of *trolls* (ogres or monsters).

2 Tell the children to imagine the Hall of the Mountain King. Ask them *Will he be a kind king or an angry king?*

3 Draw their attention to the sentence stems on the board. Then play the music (which is five minutes in length). While the music is playing, the children are using the sentence stems to write sentences about what is happening in the story.

4 The children read their sentences to their partner.

Note: Narratives are often written in the past tense, but in this case, the children are writing 'in the present' as the music suggests the action of the story.

Follow-up

- Ask the children to write and illustrate the Peer Gynt narrative. In this activity, they could change their simple present / present continuous tense sentences into a past tense narrative, and even include some dialogue.
- Other music which is suitable for this kind of activity includes:

  The William Tell Overture by Rossini
  The Nutcracker by Tchaikovsky
  Carnival of the Animals by Saint-Saens
  Peter and the Wolf by Prokofiev

- For other narratives, see Activities 2.16, 3.5, 3.13, 3.14, 3.18, 4.10, 5.1.

Box 129 The Hall of the Mountain King

Sentence stems	Sample answers
The Hall of the Mountain King looks like . . .	The Hall of the Mountain King looks like a dark cave / a cave in the jungle / an underwater world / an underground planet.
Peer Gynt is . . . into the Hall of the Mountain King.	Peer Gynt is climbing / looking / moving / walking . . .
The trolls are . . .	The trolls are running / following / jumping / kicking.
The Mountain King is . . . Peer Gynt.	The Mountain King is laughing at / shouting at / catching / throwing a pineapple / coconut / watermelon at . . .

Website appendix

These website links are correct and active at the time of going to press.

Chapter 1   Animals
Activity 1.5 To hear the melody of *Old Macdonald had a farm*, go to the British Council website. Go to 'Songs' and choose 'Little kids'. www.britishcouncil.org/kids
Activity 1.6 To find more information about writing Haiku, go to this website: www.toyomasu.com/haiku
Activity 1.17 A song about a zoo can be found at the British Council website. Go to 'Songs' and choose 'Little kids'. www.britishcouncil.org/kids

Chapter 2   Journeys
Activity 2.14 To hear this song, go to www.mudcat.org and type in 'Galway Bay'. After the printed lyrics of the song, you can 'Click to play' and listen to the melody.
Activity 2.16 For further story ideas about space, go to the British Council website. Go to 'Topics' and choose 'Space'. This site has stories for the children to read as well as a 'Story maker' where children can create their own stories. www.britishcouncil.org/kids
Activity 2.18 To hear a song about the solar system, go to the British Council website and click on 'Easy songs'. www.britishcouncil.org/kids

Chapter 3   Fantasy and adventure
Activity 3.12 A wide range of fairy tales by Hans Christian Anderson can be found on the following website: www.hca.gilead.org.il
Activity 3.13 The children can read and listen to the complete story of *Jack and the beanstalk* at the British Council website. Go to 'Stories' and click on 'Fairy Tales'. www.britishcouncil.org/kids
Activity 3.14 For other fairy stories, go to the British Council website. Go to 'Stories' and click on 'Fairy Tales'. www.britishcouncil.org/kids

Chapter 4   The world around us

Activity 4.1 If the children have access to a computer, the following website is ideal for locating a range of countries and geographical features: www.go.hrw.com/atlas/norm_htm/world.htm

Activity 4.12 The idea for the activity Ant, person, elephant came from a website about Indonesian customs and culture: www.expat.or.id/info/games.html

Chapter 5   Healthy bodies

Activity 5.1 At the British Council website, the children can listen to the complete story of *Little Red Riding Hood*. There are also a number of games connected to the story. The children could retell the story using finger puppets which can be printed from the site. Go to 'Stories' and click on 'Fairy Tales'. www.britishcouncil.org/kids

Activity 5.4 To hear the melody of the song *I have a dog and my dog loves me*, go to www.songsforteaching.com Click on 'Song lyrics' under 'English: ESL – EFL – ESOL' and choose 'My animals'.

Chapter 6   About me

Activity 6.7 To hear the melody of this song, go to www.mudcat.org and type in 'Edelweiss'.

Index

NOTE: References in **bold** type refer to Activities.

Index

Have you tried our Cambridge Copy Collection titles for young learners?

These photocopiable resource books contain a wealth of exciting games and activities for the primary classroom.

ISBN 978-0-521-54545-7

ISBN 978-0-521-54988-2

ISBN 978-0-521-54987-5

ISBN 978-0-521-77941-8

ISBN 978-0-521-00963-8

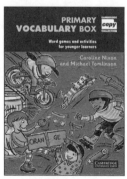

ISBN 978-0-521-52033-1

CAMBRIDGE

Three
FUN
ways to get
ready for YLE

CAMBRIDGE

FUN
for
Starters
Student's Book
ISBN 978-0-521-61358-3

CAMBRIDGE

FUN
for
Movers
Student's Book
ISBN 978-0-521-61362-0

CAMBRIDGE

FUN
for
Flyers
Student's Book
ISBN 978-0-521-61366-8

Cambridge Books for Cambridge Exams •••

- Full-colour preparation material for the updated 2007 tests
- Fun activities and exam-style questions
- Complete coverage of YLE grammar and vocabulary
- Also suitable as supplementary material for general English classes

www.cambridge.org/elt/exams

CAMBRIDGE
UNIVERSITY PRESS

CAMBRIDGE

A learning adventure

Cambridge
Storybooks

www.cambridge.org/elt/storybooks